HOW TO SPEAK FREELY

ANCIENT WISDOM FOR MODERN READERS

■ ■ ■ ■ ■

For a full list of titles in the series, go to https://press.princeton.edu/series/ancient-wisdom-for-modern-readers.

How to Speak Freely: An Ancient Guide to Free Speech and Dissent by Plato

How to Face the End of the World: An Ancient Guide for Apocalyptic Times by Lucretius, Seneca & Other Doomscrollers

How to Be Stoic: An Ancient Guide to Keeping Calm by Marcus Aurelius

How to Live: An Ancient Guide to a Happy Life by Seneca

How to Travel: An Ancient Guide for the Modern Tourist by Herodotus and Fellow Travelers

How to Listen: An Ancient Guide to Learning from Others by Plutarch

How to Compete: An Ancient Guide to the Virtues of Sports by Lucian

How to Find Happiness: An Ancient Guide to the Good Life by Marcus Tullius Cicero

How to Be Grateful: An Aztec Guide to the Art of Gratitude by Pablo of Texcoco

How to Cope: An Ancient Guide to Enduring Hardship by Boethius

How to Feel: An Ancient Guide to Minding Our Emotions by the Buddha

How to Be Caring: An Ancient Guide to a Compassionate Life by Shantideva

How to Make a Home: An Ancient Guide to Style and Comfort by Vitruvius and Guests

HOW TO SPEAK FREELY

■ ■ ■ ■ ■ ■

An Ancient Guide to Free Speech and Dissent

Plato

The Apology of Socrates

Selected, translated, and introduced by Michael Fontaine

PRINCETON UNIVERSITY PRESS
PRINCETON AND OXFORD

Published by Princeton University Press
41 William Street, Princeton, New Jersey 08540
99 Banbury Road, Oxford OX2 6JX

press.princeton.edu

GPSR Authorized Representative:
Easy Access System Europe - Mustamäe tee 50, 10621
Tallinn, Estonia, gpsr.requests@easproject.com

ISBN 978-0-691-27146-0
ISBN (epub) 978-0-691-29481-0
ISBN (PDF) 978-0-691-27149-1

Library of Congress Control Number: 2026939116

British Library Cataloging-in-Publication Data is available

Editorial: Rob Tempio and Chloe Coy
Production Editorial: Kathleen Cioffi
Text and Jacket Design: Heather Hansen
Production: Erin Suydam
Publicity: William Pagdatoon
Copyeditor: Lachlan Brooks

Jacket image: Jacques-Louis David, *The Death of Socrates*, 1787, oil on canvas, Metropolitan Museum of Art.

Gadfly icon: Anditii Creative

This book has been composed in Stempel Garamond

Printed in the United States of America

1 3 5 7 9 10 8 6 4 2

Regis quisque intra se animum habet, ut licentiam sibi dari velit, in se nolit.

Each of us has the spirit of a king inside us: we want total freedom to be granted to us but not to those acting against us.

—SENECA, *On Anger* 2.31.3
(trans. James Romm)

CONTENTS

ACKNOWLEDGMENTS

In 1749, while sitting in prison for writings deemed blasphemous and atheistic, the Enlightenment philosopher Denis Diderot (1713–84) passed the time by translating Plato's *Apology* into French. He scraped slate dust from a roof tile, mixed it with wine to make ink, and fashioned a pen from a toothpick. It was the only translation of Plato he ever undertook—an act at once symbolic and self-revealing.

The translation that follows was carried out under happier circumstances, and no wine was used for ink. Yet all around the world, freedom of speech is falling from favor. Tolerance is out; other values are in. So I hope that any authority figure who reads this book—and who may be tempted to forbid dissent on "settled" or offensive questions—will ponder a maxim of John Stuart Mill (1806–73): *All silencing of discussion is an assumption of infallibility.*

I would like to thank Rob Tempio, whose idea it was to do this and for letting me speak freely, and

Hayden Pelliccia, who helped me polish my translation. As always, I'm grateful to George Thomas for his encouragement, insight, example, and good cheer.

After Socrates himself, history's greatest gadfly is Thomas Paine (1737–1809). True to his name (for "Paine" comes from Latin *paganus*, "infidel"), he proved that plain speech has the power to liberate minds and begin the world over again. On the 250th anniversary of *Common Sense*, I dedicate this translation to his spirit.

Ithaca, New York

INTRODUCTION

Free speech is a legacy of ancient Greece. Like democracy itself, the idea that the mailed fist of government should *not* get to silence you first emerged in classical Athens. This idea was pioneering and radical and new, and it flourished during the famous fifth century BCE. This was the time of the Parthenon and Pericles, of comedy and tragedy, of history and philosophy, and the beginnings of scientific thought. Free speech soon became a civic virtue (or, as we say today, "our strength"). In public assemblies and private gatherings, male citizens were given wide latitude to express their opinions, to support or criticize each other's ideas, and to name and shame the sweaty strivers that aspired to lead them. At community-wide festival performances, meanwhile, the carnivalesque characters of stage comedy routinely broke the fourth wall to comment on current politics. Elites—often sitting right there in the audience—could suddenly find themselves the target of stinging abuse and humiliating jokes

or even parodied at great length. (The comedies of Aristophanes, whom we'll meet soon enough in these pages, are shot through with examples.) And they were expected to grin and bear it.

This critical, freewheeling spirit was considered a core component of democratic ideology, as the best way to surface and sift ideas and secure the best course of action for the community. It was part of the culture rather than a liberty enshrined in law, and it was a point of Athenian pride.

In theory, free speech in Athens came in two varieties. The first was *parrhesia*, the freedom to say pretty much anything you want in public and private life—to assess things candidly, frankly, and to speak your truth without fear. The word comes from *pan* (everything) and *rhesia*, which denotes speech (it's the root of *rhetoric*). In Latin this term was later translated *oratio libera* or *licentia*, "free speech" or "speaking freely."[1]

The second variety was *isegoria*, the freedom to have your say, to be given a platform to speak and the opportunity to be heard in the public assembly. All eligible male citizens were equally entitled to it. Hence the etymology, a combination of *iso-*, meaning "equal" (as in *isosceles*) and *-egoria*, again denoting speech, often in an assembly or marketplace (*agora*).

This theoretical distinction between *speaking* and *being platformed* sounds nice, but as the two texts in this volume demonstrate, it tends to collapse in practice and become a distinction without a difference. And twenty-five centuries later, whether online or in the workplace, it's a problem we're still grappling with today.

There is, of course, plenty of room for disagreement about how well *isegoria* and *parrhesia* align with free speech as it's understood today, whether defined narrowly under the First Amendment to the US Constitution or interpreted more expansively to include academic freedom, intellectual autonomy, and resistance to social-level pressure (for example, demands for dismissal or exclusion from a community). Ultimately, however, if free speech is binary—you either get to speak or you don't—then these ancient texts sensitize us to a truth that few pause to consider: *popular speech needs no defense.* Why would it? Always and forever, it's only *unpopular* speech—outrageous, infuriating, hurtful, "hateful" speech—that demands protection. Only when such speech is heard can we truly know whether we have free speech. Only then—and no sooner.

Our main text, Plato's *Apology of Socrates*, is a founding document of Western civilization. It

ranks as one of ancient Greece's greatest literary and philosophical achievements, a classic that everyone should read. In it, Socrates embodies the archetype of a man who thinks for himself: one of conviction who pursued his curiosity honestly, became convinced of unpopular truths, spoke candidly about them, and refused to grovel, pander, or recant—even to save his own life. By insisting on his mission and accepting the consequences, he became the most famous martyr to free inquiry in history. Here we encounter the immortal image of Socrates as a gadfly, the Socrates who declares that "the unexamined life is not worth living." And here we'll hear his account of the mysterious "voice" that allegedly guided his course in life.

The author, Plato (427–347 BCE), is the Greek philosopher par excellence: the disciple of Socrates, teacher of Aristotle, and intellectual ancestor of the West. In Athens, he founded the Academy, one of history's first universities. His dialogues, packaged as dramatic conversations among actual historical figures, explore justice, ethics, politics, and metaphysics, and they champion reason over revelation or the say-so from anyone on high. They've shaped our world ever since; as the cliché has it, all of Western philosophy really is but a series of footnotes to Plato.

Our bonus text, by Lucian of Samosata (c. 125–80 CE), is a fable on free speech told from a different angle. The Olympian gods gather in heaven for a dramatic dialogue that demonstrates how the distinction between giving someone a platform (*isegoria*) and allowing them to use it (*parrhesia*) is often only an illusion. The story also forces us to ask what we'll do ourselves when we promise free speech—and then someone takes us at our word. I'll say more about it when we get there.

> ἐρωτηθεὶς τί κάλλιστον ἐν ἀνθρώποις, ἔφη, "παρρησία."
>
> Asked what the best thing in life is, Diogenes [the Cynic] replied, "parrhesia."
>
> —DIOGENES LAERTIUS 6.69

Seeing his mentor put to death shook Plato to the core. Before they met, Plato had planned a career as a tragedian. His encounter with Socrates transformed him, redirecting his ambitions from writing plays to writing philosophy. Yet that early training appears to be the secret to his success. Unlike the lectures or articles or sermons you or I might write, Plato's

"dialogues" are essentially philosophical tragedies with the choruses left out. They're meant to come alive in our minds as we read them, much as Greek mythology comes alive before our eyes when we watch Sophocles's Oedipus feverishly race around the stage, begging and pleading and demanding to know who killed his father. Plato's *Apology of Socrates* is packed with the same kind of irony.

A word about Plato's title is in order. In the long passage from ancient Greek to modern English, many words have changed their meaning. *Hypocrite* originally meant *actor*, an *idiot* was a *private citizen*, and *heresy* meant nothing more than *choice*. The same goes for *martyr* (trial witness), *angel* (messenger), *diabolical* (slanderous), and *demon* (a spirit, not inherently evil). Yet no Greek word has changed its meaning more than "apology" itself. Today it means saying you're sorry, but originally it meant the opposite—an *apology* was a defense, a justification, an apologia, a long accounting and explanation of precisely why you are *not* sorry for what you've done. This is the sense in which Plato and Socrates intend the word.

It's said that a person with a watch knows what time it is, but a person with two is never sure. If all we had was Plato's *Apology*, we'd assume it's an accurate record of what Socrates said that fateful

day in court. Unfortunately, another follower of Socrates left us his own *Apology of Socrates*, and it's different. That author, a writer named Xenophon (430–354 BCE), was a less gifted contemporary of Plato's. That presents a problem. Plato's *Apology* is one of the most thrilling and idealistic speeches ever put to paper. Xenophon's *Apology* isn't. It's prosaic, plodding, grounded in real-world concerns. On balance, then, it's a good guess that Xenophon's *Apology* is closer to what Socrates actually said—but like the person with two watches, we can never be sure. We don't even have any idea how long after the trial Plato wrote it.

What we can be sure of, though, is that Plato's *Apology* is not a trial transcript. It is historical fiction, a spiritual rehearing of the case. The trial is over; the man is dead; now the moral reckoning can begin. Yet it's even more than that. Like a Greek tragedy, the *Apology* has immediate *practical* application in modern contexts, and that's what gives the speech transcendent value. As Aristotle observed, poetry—by which he meant fiction—is more valuable than simple history:

> The historian tells us what has happened, the poet what could happen. This is why poetry is more like philosophy and is more important

> than history. Poetry is about universals, while history is about particulars. A universal is what people would probably or necessarily say or do in a certain situation. Poetry does this even when it attaches a real name to a character, but history deals strictly with the actions or experiences of a particular person.[2]

To a greater degree than many realize, this universal quality of Plato's speech was appreciated, or at least suspected, in antiquity. "Plato," observed Dionysius of Halicarnassus (first century BCE), the foremost Greek historian and literary critic of Augustan Rome,

> does have one judicial speech to his credit: the *Apology of Socrates*. But it never so much as saw the front door of a courtroom or assembly. It was written for a different purpose, and it doesn't really qualify as either a speech or a dialogue.[3]

Even more perceptive are the observations of another Greek critic whose name and date have been lost to the vicissitudes of history (he probably lived a century or two later). This later critic wrote a treatise on *The Art of Rhetoric*, and in it he shrewdly identified and teased out the multiple interwoven

agendas the speech serves. In his view, Plato so subtly and seamlessly integrates the themes of defense, denunciation, deliberation, and self-praise that the speech encompasses every branch of oratory—and indeed, it goes beyond. "As the title indicates," he explains,

> the *Apology of Socrates* is set up as a defense speech, yet it doubles as a *J'accuse!* against the Athenians for bringing a man like himself to trial. The underlying bitterness of that accusation is concealed by the restrained character of the defense: in defending himself, Socrates effectively indicts the Athenians.[4]

That's two motifs, he says, but Plato's artistry doesn't end there. He also has Socrates implicitly praise "himself"—and yet he frames the tribute not as vainglory, but as a position the defendant is forced into by the circumstances:

> The speech also doubles as an encomium of Socrates, its offensiveness overshadowed by the necessity of self-defense. That's motif three, and hence we get two judicial themes—the defense and the accusation—integrated with one laudatory one, the praise of Socrates.

Last but not least, our critic notes, the *Apology* manages to transcend history by layering in an ideal to live up to, and an implicit call for us to live up to it:

> A fourth motif—and which was, for Plato, the most important—brings together the power of deliberative oratory with a philosophical vision, for the book is a summons to what an independent thinker ought to be. In rhetorical terms, this is called a "deliberative" idea; in philosophical terms, it's "propounding a belief"—namely, that the man or woman who values independent thought should be as Socrates appears in the *Apology*.

Whoever wrote this analysis was spot on—and prophetic. Plato's mythmaking in the *Apology* did have this effect. It elevated Socrates from a real man in history to a monumental legend. Thanks to this speech, Socrates's image narrowed in time into that of a paradigmatic martyr crushed by injustice, overshadowing the rest of his character. Frequently citing the *Apology*, the Stoics enshrined his trial and execution as the ultimate act of moral courage and the defining mark of his life. During the Enlightenment, Socrates was embraced as the archetypal victim of fanaticism and religious orthodoxy. Influ-

ential voices canonized him as the pagan saint of a new intellectual "church" devoted to free inquiry. Ever since, whenever institutions enforce ideology or suppress dissent, Socrates reappears as the enduring emblem of critical thought, martyrdom, and intellectual freedom.

So—you're surely wondering—what actually did happen? And why?

> *Ut quis destrictior accusator, velut sacrosanctus erat.*
>
> The more censorious an accuser was, the more he was virtually sacrosanct.
>
> —TACITUS, *Annals* 4.36

One day in 399 BCE, Socrates—a stonemason by trade, reportedly, though surely retired by now—was asked to come in for a meeting. Someone had filed charges against him for something he'd said, a higher-up had given it the go-ahead, and he was being called in to explain himself. This wasn't just a workplace problem, though. This was the government, and he was in serious trouble. (Plato later

dramatized this day in a dialogue titled *Euthyphro*.) He was told there was sufficient evidence against him, so his case was going to go to trial.

It did, and the prosecution won. A month later in a jail cell in Athens, Socrates lifted a cup of poison hemlock to his lips, bid his friends goodbye, and swallowed. He was seventy years old.

Before the era of "woke," we had "political correctness." Today, that latter term is a dead metaphor. Yet in classical Athens, to be out of step with the polis—to be *politically incorrect*—was literally a matter of life and death.

What could he have said to deserve this? According to the complaint—and Socrates cites it in the *Apology*—there were three issues. First, it seems he had been overheard "denying" an official (orthodox) truth. Then there was something about "idolatry," and then something vague—and perhaps sexual—about "brainwashing" or "defiling" or "perverting" young men. These three items were subsumed under the formal charge of "impiety" (in Greek, *asebeia*).

What is impiety? This once-frightening word isn't much heard today and certainly doesn't chill the blood as it once did. In previous eras it stood for blasphemy, heresy, sacrilege, satanism, profanation, apostasy, and other forms of god-offending

wickedness (a word itself derived from *wicca*, "witch").

Of all these wrongs, blasphemy may be the most unsettling. It harms not by touching anyone or anything, but by merely refusing the reverence a community accords its gods or sacred beliefs. And yet it consists of nothing more than speech (the Greek root *pheme* denotes "utterance" or "report").

In the Middle Ages and Renaissance blasphemy ranged from mocking deities or advocating heterodox views to declaring simply: "I have weighed the evidence and find it unpersuasive. It looks wrong to me." Because many believed a single miscreant could invite divine wrath upon everyone, blasphemy was treated as a matter of public health. Ideas spread as readily as infectious diseases, so communities repeatedly resorted to drastic containment measures: the cell, the rack, the crucifix—and if necessary, the stake.

Impiety is no longer a crime in most of the West, but blasphemy laws are alive and well elsewhere—and growing. As of this writing, just under half the world's countries and territories have them, with penalties ranging from fines or lashings to imprisonment and execution. (Twenty-two countries also ban apostasy, meaning you aren't even allowed to quit your religion.) These laws are on the books

and enforced in virtually every Muslim-majority country in the world, and people are sitting on death row right now for impiety. Suffice to say, for at least two billion people today—that is, a quarter of the world's population—freedom of speech simply does not exist.[5]

The religious atmosphere was not nearly so bad in classical Athens. Unlike Islam, Judaism, and Christianity, the Athenian state religion had no sacred text, so there was no creed to subscribe to. For the most part, orthodoxy—correct thinking—had to be inferred from "orthopraxy," which meant proper observance of communal rituals, such as participating in state festivals and animal sacrifice. The only other way was to ask someone his or her opinions. But since lying was always an option—and since there were no scriptures one even *could* contradict or blaspheme—this situation surely explains why in classical Athens, prosecutions for impiety were mostly rare and seemingly opportunistic.

In religious societies, impiety means blasphemy against the gods or God or His representatives here on earth. Yet Plato's *Apology* helps us see how the concept survives in secular times. In post-religious societies, impiety has been replaced by the successor crimes of hate speech, which is blasphemy against sacrosanct minorities, and Holocaust denial, which

is blasphemy against a sacralized event. Doubts or dissent about either are typically seen as in league with evil, so communities resort to drastic containment measures. In many liberal democracies a conviction for either crime will get you locked up, and "truth"—that is, your honest assessment of the data that you regard as relevant—is not an allowable defense.

No one has documented the historical transition from theological impiety to secular impiety more compellingly than Thomas Szasz (1920–2012), the Hungarian American psychiatrist and last true Enlightenment thinker. Whenever the individual is at odds with the collective, he notes, some form of heresy exists, but what qualifies as heresy changes over time. In an era when Christian doctrine defined communal order, heresy meant deviation from the Church's dogmas. In an era held together by science, medicine, and health, heresy takes the form of dissent from the prevailing wisdom of scientists and doctors.[6] And in a liberal democracy, expressions of illiberalism will invariably appear as heresy—and, therefore, potentially fatal to the community.

This is the crucial point to grasp about the predicament Socrates found himself in. In an autocracy, truth is a matter of decree: authority tells you what you can and cannot say. (As the joke has it, a man

from North Korea was asked what his country is really like. He said he can't complain.) In a free society, by contrast, what counts as the truth is up to us. The problem, suggests Socrates—and this is the core insight he strives to impress on us in his defense—is that when it comes to most matters in this world, what do you or I or any of us really and truly *know*? What do we know that doesn't somehow rely on hearsay or a leap of faith? The answer is, very little. And under such circumstances, Socrates implies, a free society should not impose criminal penalties for questioning dogma.

In any case, the point is not whether Socrates or any other heretic is objectively right or wrong. The point is whether the state or community is morally right to insist that he acknowledge the truth, and to silence or kill him if he won't.

In this context, it's easy to link the three accusations against Socrates together. Take, for instance, the charge of "idolatry." As he discusses in the speech, Socrates was accused of believing in "new" or "kooky" (for the word in question, *kainos*, means both) gods that the city does not grant credence to.[7] This charge seems to go hand in glove with his alleged "denial" of the city's gods, much as one might reject Christianity for another religion or Western science in favor of alternative medicine. Both charges

also fit in well with the third item in the complaint—"brainwashing the youth"—because in classical Athens, impiety was thought to be contagious. If left unchecked, a dangerous "miasma" could spread throughout the community and compromise others.

As we'll see in the speech, Socrates answers all three charges. He doesn't link them in this way, and it's hard to tell whether his accusers did either. But before you reassure yourself that you'd have voted to acquit him, consider how many of his contemporaries must have viewed him: essentially as a Holocaust denier, a racist, perhaps even a crypto-Nazi in their midst.

This reflection brings us to his impact on the community and the political climate in which his trial took place.

> But the accuser said, "Critias and Alcibiades had been associates of Socrates, and those two did the city enormous harm. Critias became the most grasping and violent of all those in the oligarchy, and Alcibiades was the most irresponsible and abusive of all those in the democracy."
>
> —XENOPHON, *Memories of Socrates* 1.12

INTRODUCTION

It's often said that Athens in the fifth century BCE was a democracy—for its male citizens, anyway—but that was true only back home in the city itself. Everywhere else it ruled over a restive empire, and it spent the last third of the century locked in endless war with Sparta and its allies. When Athens finally lost, its democracy was dismantled and replaced by a puppet regime installed by Sparta. Thirty Athenian men, tasked with reimagining the state along Spartan lines, soon unleashed a brief but brutal reign of terror. They—"The Thirty"—purged some 1,500 of their fellow citizens without trial, and would have executed more if not for a brief civil war. A hero named Thrasybulus led the resistance, and a single battle ended the regime. The leader of The Thirty, Critias, was killed, and democracy restored. The year was 403 BCE, just four years before Socrates received his summons. It was a fragile era of reconstruction, and it was not at all certain that democracy would survive.

An intellectual turned oligarch, Critias (c. 460–403 BCE) is a tantalizing figure. An outright atheist, he dismissed religion as a cynical invention of man designed for social control. In forty-two lines of Greek verse, his explosive "Sisyphus fragment" declares that the gods were invented to terrorize the masses, enforce morality, and that "some wise and shrewd man began promoting this doctrine, this lie,

as if it were true."[8] In political life, he became the Robespierre of ancient Athens. Once in power, he justified terror with virtue and subscribed to Stalin's alleged maxim: "No man, no problem."

That's bad enough, of course, but worse is that Critias and a turncoat general named Alcibiades had once been associates of Socrates. (Socrates never mentions either man in Plato's *Apology*, perhaps because Critias was a relative of Plato's.)

Socrates himself faced three accusers. The most prominent, Meletus, is a familiar type. He was an ambitious young activist with no wealth or influence of his own but a hunger for both. Taking Socrates down would be his ticket to power. He takes the leading role in the trial.[9]

Meletus made himself the willing pawn of the second accuser, Anytus. Anytus was a wealthy and powerful pro-democracy politician and the evident mastermind of the operation. (Reflecting this influence, Roman poets in later centuries simply refer to Socrates as *reus Anyti*, "Anytus's respondent."[10]) Under The Thirty, he'd been forced into exile and saw his vast property plundered by the state. Some believe that in seeking the death penalty for Socrates, Anytus merely hoped to terrify the old man into fleeing Athens before the trial commenced. If so, he thought wrong.

The third accuser, Lycon, is mostly a mystery. All we know is that his son, an impressive Olympic athlete, had been killed by The Thirty.

Thanks to a recent government decree—an "amnesty"—all such horrors were officially "forgotten" by the time of Socrates's trial. No one was supposed to be prosecuted for involvement in the reign of The Thirty. But exile or the death of a son is not easily forgotten, nor are those responsible. Understandably, some blamed Socrates for his purported followers' actions.

Since antiquity, some have suspected this political background was the real reason for Socrates's trial, conviction, and execution. If so, it remains impossible to prove. As the notes to this edition suggest, however, the endlessly recurring echoes of his ordeal in Western history—from the charges to the sentencing—make the hypothesis unnecessary, even if it may ultimately be true.

What transpired on his fateful day in court? Socrates stood trial before a jury of five hundred Athenian citizens, who alone determined his fate—there was no independent judge. The entire trial was required to conclude within a single day. The process was swift: the prosecution presented its case and called witnesses, followed by Socrates's rebuttal. After hearing both sides, the jury voted and found

him guilty. The prosecution then proposed a penalty, the defense offered an alternative, and the jury chose between them.

Plato's *Apology* will make all this clear and more. Step by step, it maps Socrates's collision course with his city. And it shows us how, in a democracy, a gadfly could be convicted for his convictions, and put to death for thinking for himself.

And therein lay some important lessons for us.

> All truth passes through three stages. First, it is ridiculed, then it is violently opposed, and finally it is accepted as self-evident.
>
> —ARTHUR SCHOPENHAUER
> (1819, xvi, translator unknown)

Any reader of Socrates's speech will soon realize that the modern-day dissenter faces an age-old dilemma. Writing in the midst of the culture wars of the 1990s, Thomas Szasz pointed out the paradox of education in a free society. "It is dangerous to speak plainly and to tell the truth," observed Szasz, and not just in religious or totalitarian societies: "We ceaselessly exhort young men and women to think for themselves. However, when they do, their

thoughts—and hence what they say and write—are likely to differ from what passes as politically correct.... What, then, are young men and young women to do when they heed the advice to think for themselves and arrive at thoughts that differ from what passes as politically correct?"[11] It's an excellent question. When *impolite* and *impolitic* become synonymous, what *should* you do?

One option is to bite your tongue and play along—forever. Atheists have surely sat in pews all through history, so you could follow in their footsteps. The problem is that most of us find it unbearably hard to grit our teeth. We crave self-expression.

Another is to hedge and prevaricate and play a double game—forever. The problem is that most of us find it unbearably hard to live a lie. We crave honesty and trust and integrity.

That leaves us the Socrates option: speak your truth boldly, consequences be damned. If you win the day, you'll shatter some illusion and change society for the better. If you don't—if the Meletuses and Anytuses of your time make sure you go down in flames—you'll join the glorious ranks of martyrs who spoke truth to power before you.

What will you do?

THE APOLOGY OF SOCRATES

PLATO

ΑΠΟΛΟΓΙΑ ΣΩΚΡΑΤΟΥΣ

ΠΛΑΤΩΝΟΣ

[17a] ὅτι μὲν ὑμεῖς, ὦ ἄνδρες Ἀθηναῖοι, πεπόνθατε ὑπὸ τῶν ἐμῶν κατηγόρων, οὐκ οἶδα· ἐγὼ δ' οὖν καὶ αὐτὸς ὑπ' αὐτῶν ὀλίγου ἐμαυτοῦ ἐπελαθόμην, οὕτω πιθανῶς ἔλεγον. καίτοι ἀληθές γε ὡς ἔπος εἰπεῖν οὐδὲν εἰρήκασιν. μάλιστα δὲ αὐτῶν ἓν ἐθαύμασα τῶν πολλῶν ὧν ἐψεύσαντο, τοῦτο ἐν ᾧ ἔλεγον ὡς χρῆν ὑμᾶς εὐλαβεῖσθαι μὴ ὑπ' ἐμοῦ ἐξαπατηθῆτε [17b] ὡς δεινοῦ ὄντος λέγειν. τὸ γὰρ μὴ αἰσχυνθῆναι ὅτι αὐτίκα ὑπ' ἐμοῦ ἐξελεγχθήσονται ἔργῳ, ἐπειδὰν μηδ' ὁπωστιοῦν φαίνωμαι δεινὸς λέγειν, τοῦτό μοι ἔδοξεν αὐτῶν ἀναισχυντότατον εἶναι, εἰ μὴ ἄρα δεινὸν καλοῦσιν οὗτοι λέγειν τὸν τἀληθῆ λέγοντα· εἰ μὲν γὰρ τοῦτο λέγουσιν, ὁμολογοίην ἂν ἔγωγε οὐ κατὰ τούτους εἶναι ῥήτωρ.

οὗτοι μὲν οὖν, ὥσπερ ἐγὼ λέγω, ἤ τι ἢ οὐδὲν ἀληθὲς εἰρήκασιν, ὑμεῖς δέ μου ἀκούσεσθε πᾶσαν τὴν ἀλήθειαν—οὐ μέντοι μὰ Δία, ὦ ἄνδρες Ἀθηναῖοι, κεκαλλιεπημένους γε λόγους, [17c] ὥσπερ οἱ τούτων,

THE APOLOGY OF SOCRATES

PLATO

[17a] I don't know what impression my accusers made on you, men of Athens, but I for one got so carried away that I almost forgot who I am! They really were that good. And yet almost nothing they said was true. Out of all the lies they told, though, one stood out the most—when they warned you to watch out and not let me fool you [17b] because I'm some "dangerously clever" speaker. The audacity of that one amazed me, because once I explain the facts and it emerges that I'm not even close to being a dangerously clever speaker, their claim will look shameless to the core. Unless, of course, that expression "dangerously clever" just means someone who speaks the truth—because if that's the case, then I agree: I *am* an orator, just not in the sense that they'd define that word.

Anyway, as I was saying, while they barely said a word that's true, I'm going to tell you the whole truth. But I certainly won't do it in some fancy-dancy speech [17c] like theirs, gentlemen of Athens,

ῥήμασί τε καὶ ὀνόμασιν οὐδὲ κεκοσμημένους, ἀλλ᾽ ἀκούσεσθε εἰκῇ λεγόμενα τοῖς ἐπιτυχοῦσιν ὀνόμασιν—πιστεύω γὰρ δίκαια εἶναι ἃ λέγω—καὶ μηδεὶς ὑμῶν προσδοκησάτω ἄλλως· οὐδὲ γὰρ ἂν δήπου πρέποι, ὦ ἄνδρες, τῇδε τῇ ἡλικίᾳ ὥσπερ μειρακίῳ πλάττοντι λόγους εἰς ὑμᾶς εἰσιέναι.

καὶ μέντοι καὶ πάνυ, ὦ ἄνδρες Ἀθηναῖοι, τοῦτο ὑμῶν δέομαι καὶ παρίεμαι· ἐὰν διὰ τῶν αὐτῶν λόγων ἀκούητέ μου ἀπολογουμένου δι᾽ ὧνπερ εἴωθα λέγειν καὶ ἐν ἀγορᾷ ἐπὶ τῶν τραπεζῶν, ἵνα ὑμῶν πολλοὶ ἀκηκόασι, καὶ ἄλλοθι, μήτε θαυμάζειν μήτε θορυβεῖν τούτου ἕνεκα. ἔχει γὰρ οὑτωσί. [17d] νῦν ἐγὼ πρῶτον ἐπὶ δικαστήριον ἀναβέβηκα, ἔτη γεγονὼς ἑβδομήκοντα· ἀτεχνῶς οὖν ξένως ἔχω τῆς ἐνθάδε λέξεως. ὥσπερ οὖν ἄν, εἰ τῷ ὄντι ξένος ἐτύγχανον ὤν, συνεγιγνώσκετε δήπου ἄν μοι εἰ ἐν ἐκείνῃ τῇ φωνῇ τε καὶ τῷ τρόπῳ ἔλεγον ἐν οἷσπερ ἐτεθράμμην, [18a] καὶ δὴ καὶ νῦν τοῦτο ὑμῶν δέομαι δίκαιον, ὥς γέ μοι δοκῶ, τὸν μὲν τρόπον τῆς λέξεως ἐᾶν—ἴσως μὲν γὰρ χείρων, ἴσως δὲ βελτίων ἂν εἴη—αὐτὸ δὲ τοῦτο σκοπεῖν καὶ τούτῳ τὸν νοῦν προσέχειν, εἰ δίκαια λέγω ἢ μή· δικαστοῦ μὲν γὰρ αὕτη ἀρετή, ῥήτορος δὲ τἀληθῆ λέγειν.

πρῶτον μὲν οὖν δίκαιός εἰμι ἀπολογήσασθαι, ὦ ἄνδρες Ἀθηναῖοι, πρὸς τὰ πρῶτά μου ψευδῆ

all full of artful flourishes and catchy wordplay. No, you'll hear me speaking in plain old Greek, off the cuff, with whatever words come to mind, because I trust in the justice of what I'm saying. And honestly, not a one of you should expect anything else, because at my age it'd be completely absurd to show up here like some young hotshot with a pat production.

That's right, gentlemen of Athens, and in fact, I have a favor to ask: if you do hear me defending myself with the same normal words I'm always using in the marketplace out near the bankers' tables—where many of you have heard me before—or anywhere else, then don't be surprised or start jeering at me. [17d] You see, in my seventy years this is the first time I've ever appeared in court, and the language here feels completely foreign to me.[1] Now, if I really were a foreigner, I'm sure you'd bear with me if I spoke in the dialect or with the tics I grew up with. [18a] By the same reasoning, then, I ask that you disregard how I speak here—whether it's worse or better than what you're accustomed to—and focus on one thing alone: whether what I'm saying is just or not. After all, that's your job as jurors, the same way it's my job as an orator to tell the truth.

Since first things are first, gentlemen of Athens, it's only fair that I begin by defending myself

κατηγορημένα καὶ τοὺς πρώτους κατηγόρους, ἔπειτα δὲ πρὸς τὰ ὕστερον καὶ τοὺς ὑστέρους. [18b] ἐμοῦ γὰρ πολλοὶ κατήγοροι γεγόνασι πρὸς ὑμᾶς καὶ πάλαι πολλὰ ἤδη ἔτη καὶ οὐδὲν ἀληθὲς λέγοντες, οὓς ἐγὼ μᾶλλον φοβοῦμαι ἢ τοὺς ἀμφὶ Ἄνυτον, καίπερ ὄντας καὶ τούτους δεινούς· ἀλλ' ἐκεῖνοι δεινότεροι, ὦ ἄνδρες, οἳ ὑμῶν τοὺς πολλοὺς ἐκ παίδων παραλαμβάνοντες ἔπειθόν τε καὶ κατηγόρουν ἐμοῦ μᾶλλον οὐδὲν ἀληθές, ὡς

> ἔστιν τις Σωκράτης σοφὸς ἀνήρ, τά τε μετέωρα φροντιστὴς καὶ τὰ ὑπὸ γῆς πάντα ἀνεζητηκὼς καὶ τὸν [18c] ἥττω λόγον κρείττω ποιῶν.

οὗτοι, ὦ ἄνδρες Ἀθηναῖοι, <οἱ> ταύτην τὴν φήμην κατασκεδάσαντες, οἱ δεινοί εἰσίν μου κατήγοροι· οἱ γὰρ ἀκούοντες ἡγοῦνται τοὺς ταῦτα ζητοῦντας οὐδὲ θεοὺς νομίζειν. ἔπειτά εἰσιν οὗτοι οἱ κατήγοροι πολλοὶ καὶ πολὺν χρόνον ἤδη κατηγορηκότες, ἔτι δὲ καὶ ἐν ταύτῃ τῇ ἡλικίᾳ λέγοντες πρὸς ὑμᾶς ἐν ᾗ ἂν μάλιστα ἐπιστεύσατε, παῖδες ὄντες ἔνιοι ὑμῶν καὶ μειράκια, ἀτεχνῶς ἐρήμην κατηγοροῦντες ἀπολογουμένου

against my first accusers and their allegations, and then come to the more recent ones later. [18b] You see, accusers have been circulating allegations about me among you for years—many accusers, and long before this trial. None of their whispers are true, but I'm actually more afraid of them than I am of Anytus and his crew. Oh, he's certainly dangerous too, but those earlier accusers frighten me more, gentlemen, because they got to you with their false ideas about me when you were still children. They've been spreading stories like this:

> "There's this man named Socrates—a 'free-thinker.' He's a theorist of things beyond the heavens, an expert in everything beneath the earth, and he makes the weaker argument into [18c] the stronger one."

The ones who have smeared my reputation like this, gentlemen of Athens, are the truly dangerous accusers, because people hear them and assume that anyone who studies such things doesn't believe in gods. These accusers are legion, and they've been at it a long time. Worse, they got to you at your most impressionable—when some of you were still kids or teenagers—and they basically convicted me in absentia, with nobody there to defend me. And the

οὐδενός. ὃ δὲ πάντων ἀλογώτατον, ὅτι οὐδὲ τὰ ὀνόματα οἷόν τε [18d] αὐτῶν εἰδέναι καὶ εἰπεῖν, πλὴν εἴ τις κωμῳδοποιὸς τυγχάνει ὤν.

ὅσοι δὲ φθόνῳ καὶ διαβολῇ χρώμενοι ὑμᾶς ἀνέπειθον, οἱ δὲ καὶ αὐτοὶ πεπεισμένοι ἄλλους πείθοντες, οὗτοι πάντες ἀπορώτατοί εἰσιν· οὐδὲ γὰρ ἀναβιβάσασθαι οἷόν τ᾽ ἐστὶν αὐτῶν ἐνταυθοῖ οὐδ᾽ ἐλέγξαι οὐδένα, ἀλλ᾽ ἀνάγκη ἀτεχνῶς ὥσπερ σκιαμαχεῖν ἀπολογούμενόν τε καὶ ἐλέγχειν μηδενὸς ἀποκρινομένου.

ἀξιώσατε οὖν καὶ ὑμεῖς, ὥσπερ ἐγὼ λέγω, διττούς μου τοὺς κατηγόρους γεγονέναι, ἑτέρους μὲν τοὺς ἄρτι κατηγορήσαντας, ἑτέρους δὲ [18e] τοὺς πάλαι οὓς ἐγὼ λέγω, καὶ οἰήθητε δεῖν πρὸς ἐκείνους πρῶτόν με ἀπολογήσασθαι· καὶ γὰρ ὑμεῖς ἐκείνων πρότερον ἠκούσατε κατηγορούντων καὶ πολὺ μᾶλλον ἢ τῶνδε τῶν ὕστερον.

εἶεν· ἀπολογητέον δή, ὦ ἄνδρες Ἀθηναῖοι, [19a] καὶ ἐπιχειρητέον ὑμῶν ἐξελέσθαι τὴν διαβολὴν ἣν ὑμεῖς ἐν πολλῷ χρόνῳ ἔσχετε ταύτην ἐν οὕτως ὀλίγῳ χρόνῳ. βουλοίμην μὲν οὖν ἂν τοῦτο οὕτως γενέσθαι, εἴ τι ἄμεινον καὶ ὑμῖν καὶ ἐμοί, καὶ πλέον τί με ποιῆσαι ἀπολογούμενον·

οἶμαι δὲ αὐτὸ χαλεπὸν εἶναι, καὶ οὐ πάνυ με λανθάνει οἷόν ἐστιν. ὅμως τοῦτο μὲν ἴτω ὅπῃ τῷ θεῷ φίλον, τῷ δὲ νόμῳ πειστέον καὶ ἀπολογητέον.

craziest part is that I can't even tell you most of their names [18d], except for a few comic playwrights.[2]

All who prejudiced you against me with these malicious smears—and then got others to buy into them once they'd bought into them themselves—have left me in an impossible bind. There's no way to subpoena or cross-examine any of them here. I'm stuck fighting shadows—trying to defend myself by cross-examining accusers that aren't even here to answer!

So let's agree—as I've been saying—that my accusers fall into two groups: those who have accused me here in court today, and those [18e] from long ago, as I've described. And let's also agree that I must first defend myself against the earlier group, since you heard from them before you heard from the newer crowd—and moreover, you heard them far more often.

All right then—gentlemen of Athens, a defense is now in order. [19a] In the brief time we have, I'll do my utmost to challenge the biases you've accumulated over the years. Nothing would please me more than to succeed in that—both for your sake and mine—and, above all, to prevail in my defense.

But I won't pretend that this is easy. I know full well the challenge that lies before me, and I'm under no illusions about it. I leave the outcome to the god;

ἀναλάβωμεν οὖν ἐξ ἀρχῆς τίς ἡ κατηγορία ἐστὶν ἐξ ἧς [19b] ἡ ἐμὴ διαβολὴ γέγονεν, ᾗ δὴ καὶ πιστεύων Μέλητός με ἐγράψατο τὴν γραφὴν ταύτην. εἶεν· τί δὴ λέγοντες διέβαλλον οἱ διαβάλλοντες; ὥσπερ οὖν κατηγόρων τὴν ἀντωμοσίαν δεῖ ἀναγνῶναι αὐτῶν·

> "Σωκράτης ἀδικεῖ καὶ περιεργάζεται ζητῶν τά τε ὑπὸ γῆς καὶ οὐράνια καὶ τὸν [19c] ἥττω λόγον κρείττω ποιῶν καὶ ἄλλους ταὐτὰ ταῦτα διδάσκων."

τοιαύτη τίς ἐστιν· ταῦτα γὰρ ἑωρᾶτε καὶ αὐτοὶ ἐν τῇ Ἀριστοφάνους κωμῳδίᾳ, Σωκράτη τινὰ ἐκεῖ περιφερόμενον, φάσκοντά τε ἀεροβατεῖν καὶ ἄλλην

in the meantime, the law demands a defense—and defend myself I shall.*

Let us begin with the accusation that ignited all this prejudice against me [19b]—the same prejudice upon which Meletus relies in bringing this case. What exactly did the gossipmongers say to turn people against me? As with my accusers present today, we must "read" (so to speak) their "complaint" too:

> "Socrates is guilty—and a troublemaker—of investigating things beneath the earth and beyond the heavens, of making [19c] the weaker argument into the stronger one, and of teaching these things to others."

That's essentially how it goes, because it's what you saw for yourselves in Aristophanes's *Clouds*. In that comedy there's a "Socrates" swinging around on some contraption, proclaiming that he's walking

---

* Here and elsewhere Socrates refers simply to "the god," without specification. The phrase is as odd and vague in Greek as in English, suggesting anything from Apollo or Zeus to something closer to "God" or "the deity"—an ambiguity that appears calculated.

πολλὴν φλυαρίαν φλυαροῦντα, ὧν ἐγὼ οὐδὲν οὔτε μέγα οὔτε μικρὸν πέρι ἐπαΐω. καὶ οὐχ ὡς ἀτιμάζων λέγω τὴν τοιαύτην ἐπιστήμην, εἴ τις περὶ τῶν τοιούτων σοφός ἐστιν—μή πως ἐγὼ ὑπὸ Μελήτου τοσαύτας δίκας φεύγοιμι.

ἀλλὰ γὰρ ἐμοὶ τούτων, ὦ ἄνδρες Ἀθηναῖοι, [19d] οὐδὲν μέτεστιν. μάρτυρας δὲ αὖ ὑμῶν τοὺς πολλοὺς παρέχομαι, καὶ ἀξιῶ ὑμᾶς ἀλλήλους διδάσκειν τε καὶ φράζειν, ὅσοι ἐμοῦ πώποτε ἀκηκόατε διαλεγομένου—πολλοὶ δὲ ὑμῶν οἱ τοιοῦτοί εἰσιν—φράζετε οὖν ἀλλήλοις εἰ πώποτε ἢ μικρὸν ἢ μέγα ἤκουσέ τις ὑμῶν ἐμοῦ περὶ τῶν τοιούτων διαλεγομένου, καὶ ἐκ τούτου γνώσεσθε ὅτι τοιαῦτ᾽ ἐστὶ καὶ τἆλλα περὶ ἐμοῦ ἃ οἱ πολλοὶ λέγουσιν.

ἀλλὰ γὰρ οὔτε τούτων οὐδέν ἐστιν, οὐδέ γ᾽ εἴ τινος ἀκηκόατε ὡς ἐγὼ παιδεύειν ἐπιχειρῶ ἀνθρώπους καὶ χρήματα πράττομαι, [19e] οὐδὲ τοῦτο ἀληθές. ἐπεὶ καὶ τοῦτό γέ μοι δοκεῖ καλὸν εἶναι, εἴ τις οἷός τ᾽ εἴη παιδεύειν ἀνθρώπους ὥσπερ Γοργίας τε ὁ Λεοντῖνος καὶ Πρόδικος ὁ Κεῖος καὶ Ἱππίας ὁ Ἠλεῖος. τούτων γὰρ ἕκαστος, ὦ ἄνδρες, οἷός τ᾽ ἐστὶν ἰὼν εἰς ἑκάστην τῶν πόλεων τοὺς νέους, οἷς ἔξεστι τῶν ἑαυτῶν πολιτῶν προῖκα συνεῖναι ᾧ ἂν βούλωνται, [20a] τούτους

on air and spouting all kinds of nonsense—topics I don't have the faintest idea about. And when I say I have no such knowledge, I mean no offense to anyone who may genuinely understand those things. And I hope I never have to face Meletus on endless charges for *that*!

No, gentlemen, I have nothing to do [19d] with any of that. And again, I call upon the majority of you to serve as my witnesses. Talk among yourselves—all of you who have ever heard me in conversation, and there are many such of you. Go on, ask each other: has anyone ever heard me discoursing on such subjects—briefly or at length, at any time? If you do, then you'll see for yourselves how entirely baseless this gossip really is.

Socrates pauses to give the jurors time to chat.

As you can see, there's no truth to any of that. And the same goes for another rumor you may have heard—that I teach and charge for it. [19e] That isn't true either—though I must admit, if anyone *can* teach as skillfully as Gorgias of Leontini, Prodicus of Ceos, and Hippias of Elis, it really is impressive. I mean, these men arrive in city after city and persuade young people—who could associate with any citizen they like for free [20a]—to leave their old

πείθουσι τὰς ἐκείνων συνουσίας ἀπολιπόντας σφίσιν συνεῖναι χρήματα διδόντας καὶ χάριν προσειδέναι.

ἐπεὶ καὶ ἄλλος ἀνήρ ἐστι Πάριος ἐνθάδε σοφὸς ὃν ἐγὼ ᾐσθόμην ἐπιδημοῦντα· ἔτυχον γὰρ προσελθὼν ἀνδρὶ ὃς τετέλεκε χρήματα σοφισταῖς πλείω ἢ σύμπαντες οἱ ἄλλοι, Καλλίᾳ τῷ Ἱππονίκου· τοῦτον οὖν ἀνηρόμην—ἐστὸν γὰρ αὐτῷ δύο ὑεῖ—"Ὦ Καλλία," ἦν δ' ἐγώ,

"εἰ μέν σου τὼ ὑεῖ πώλω ἢ μόσχω ἐγενέσθην, εἴχομεν ἂν αὐτοῖν ἐπιστάτην λαβεῖν καὶ μισθώσασθαι ὃς ἔμελλεν αὐτὼ καλώ τε [20b] κἀγαθὼ ποιήσειν τὴν προσήκουσαν ἀρετήν· ἦν δ' ἂν οὗτος ἢ τῶν ἱππικῶν τις ἢ τῶν γεωργικῶν· νῦν δ' ἐπειδὴ ἀνθρώπω ἐστόν, τίνα αὐτοῖν ἐν νῷ ἔχεις ἐπιστάτην λαβεῖν; τίς τῆς τοιαύτης ἀρετῆς, τῆς ἀνθρωπίνης τε καὶ πολιτικῆς, ἐπιστήμων ἐστίν; οἶμαι γάρ σε ἐσκέφθαι διὰ τὴν τῶν ὑέων κτῆσιν. ἔστιν τις," ἔφην ἐγώ, "ἢ οὔ;"

"πάνυ γε," ἦ δ' ὅς.

"τίς," ἦν δ' ἐγώ, "καὶ ποδαπός, καὶ πόσου διδάσκει;"

"Εὔηνος," ἔφη, "ὦ Σώκρατες, Πάριος, πέντε μνῶν."

companions and flock to them instead. And they pay for that privilege. What irony, they even count themselves *fortunate* for the chance![3]

Speaking of which, I hear there's another knowledgeable fellow here in town, a man from Paros. You see, I happened to bump into a man who has spent more money on "intellectuals" than everyone else put together.[4] His name is Callias son of Hipponicus, and since he has two sons, I asked him about it. "Callias," I said,

> "If your sons had been born horses or cattle, we could easily find a trainer—a cowboy or rancher, someone [20b] who could turn them into fine, gentlemanly animals. But they're people. So what kind of trainer are you planning to get them? What expert—what 'mentor,' if you will—can develop *mental* potential, and shape them into good people and responsible citizens? I'm sure you've thought about it, seeing that you have the sons. Is there someone like that, or not?"[5]
>
> "There is," he replied.
>
> "Who?" I asked. "Where's he from? And what's his fee?"
>
> "Evenus of Paros," he replied, "and he charges five minas of silver."[6]

καὶ ἐγὼ τὸν Εὔηνον ἐμακάρισα εἰ ὡς ἀληθῶς ἔχοι ταύτην τὴν [20c] τέχνην καὶ οὕτως ἐμμελῶς διδάσκει. ἐγὼ γοῦν καὶ αὐτὸς ἐκαλλυνόμην τε καὶ ἡβρυνόμην ἂν εἰ ἠπιστάμην ταῦτα· ἀλλ' οὐ γὰρ ἐπίσταμαι, ὦ ἄνδρες Ἀθηναῖοι.

ὑπολάβοι ἂν οὖν τις ὑμῶν ἴσως·

"ἀλλ', ὦ Σώκρατες, τὸ σὸν τί ἐστι πρᾶγμα; πόθεν αἱ διαβολαί σοι αὗται γεγόνασιν; οὐ γὰρ δήπου σοῦ γε οὐδὲν τῶν ἄλλων περιττότερον πραγματευομένου ἔπειτα τοσαύτη φήμη τε καὶ λόγος γέγονεν, εἰ μή τι ἔπραττες ἀλλοῖον ἢ οἱ πολλοί. [20d] λέγε οὖν ἡμῖν τί ἐστιν, ἵνα μὴ ἡμεῖς περὶ σοῦ αὐτοσχεδιάζωμεν."

ταυτί μοι δοκεῖ δίκαια λέγειν ὁ λέγων, κἀγὼ ὑμῖν πειράσομαι ἀποδεῖξαι τί ποτ' ἐστὶν τοῦτο ὃ ἐμοὶ πεποίηκεν τό τε ὄνομα καὶ τὴν διαβολήν. ἀκούετε δή. καὶ ἴσως μὲν δόξω τισὶν ὑμῶν παίζειν· εὖ μέντοι ἴστε, πᾶσαν ὑμῖν τὴν ἀλήθειαν ἐρῶ.

ἐγὼ γάρ, ὦ ἄνδρες Ἀθηναῖοι, δι' οὐδὲν ἀλλ' ἢ διὰ σοφίαν τινὰ τοῦτο τὸ ὄνομα ἔσχηκα. ποίαν δὴ σοφίαν ταύτην; ἥπερ ἐστὶν ἴσως ἀνθρωπίνη σοφία· τῷ ὄντι

"Happy is Evenus," I thought, if he truly possesses this [20c] expertise, and he's selling lessons in it for such a modest price. I must say I'd be rather full of myself if I knew those things, gentlemen of Athens. But the truth is, I don't.

Now, one of you might perhaps object:

> "Very well, Socrates, what *do* you do? If you're not doing anything unusual, then where did all these smears come from? Because if you *haven't* been doing something other people don't, it's hard to believe all these rumors just came out of nowhere—unless you've been doing something most people don't. [20d] So tell us what it is, and that way we won't go jumping to conclusions about you."

That's fair—you've got a point, and I'll do my utmost to set the record straight—so listen closely: I'll explain what's behind this reputation and the prejudice against me. Now, some of you may suspect I'm joking, but let me assure you: I'll be telling you the whole truth.

You see, men of Athens, the reputation I've earned comes down to one thing—and one thing only: this notion of "wisdom." What kind of wisdom? Perhaps it's simply human wisdom, because it

γὰρ κινδυνεύω ταύτην εἶναι σοφός. οὗτοι δὲ τάχ᾽ ἄν, οὓς ἄρτι ἔλεγον, [20e] μείζω τινὰ ἢ κατ᾽ ἄνθρωπον σοφίαν σοφοὶ εἶεν, ἢ οὐκ ἔχω τί λέγω· οὐ γὰρ δὴ ἔγωγε αὐτὴν ἐπίσταμαι, ἀλλ᾽ ὅστις φησὶ ψεύδεταί τε καὶ ἐπὶ διαβολῇ τῇ ἐμῇ λέγει.

καί μοι, ὦ ἄνδρες Ἀθηναῖοι, μὴ θορυβήσητε, μηδ᾽ ἐὰν δόξω τι ὑμῖν μέγα λέγειν· οὐ γὰρ ἐμὸν ἐρῶ τὸν λόγον ὃν ἂν λέγω, ἀλλ᾽ εἰς ἀξιόχρεων ὑμῖν τὸν λέγοντα ἀνοίσω. τῆς γὰρ ἐμῆς, εἰ δή τίς ἐστιν σοφία καὶ οἵα, μάρτυρα ὑμῖν παρέξομαι τὸν θεὸν τὸν ἐν Δελφοῖς.

Χαιρεφῶντα γὰρ ἴστε που. [21a] οὗτος ἐμός τε ἑταῖρος ἦν ἐκ νέου καὶ ὑμῶν τῷ πλήθει ἑταῖρός τε καὶ συνέφυγε τὴν φυγὴν ταύτην καὶ μεθ᾽ ὑμῶν κατῆλθε. καὶ ἴστε δὴ οἷος ἦν Χαιρεφῶν, ὡς σφοδρὸς ἐφ᾽ ὅτι ὁρμήσειεν. καὶ δή ποτε καὶ εἰς Δελφοὺς ἐλθὼν ἐτόλμησε τοῦτο μαντεύσασθαι—καί, ὅπερ λέγω, μὴ θορυβεῖτε, ὦ ἄνδρες—ἤρετο γὰρ δὴ εἴ τις ἐμοῦ εἴη σοφώτερος. ἀνεῖλεν οὖν ἡ Πυθία μηδένα σοφώτερον εἶναι. καὶ τούτων πέρι ὁ ἀδελφὸς ὑμῖν αὐτοῦ οὑτοσὶ μαρτυρήσει, ἐπειδὴ ἐκεῖνος τετελεύτηκεν.

may well be that I'm wise in that sense. Maybe those others I spoke of [20e] possess a type of wisdom far beyond human ken. I'm just not sure, since I don't understand it myself, and anyone who says I do is lying and damaging my name.

And please, gentlemen of Athens—don't shout me down, even if what I say does sound a bit bold. The story I'm about to tell isn't my own, but I'm going to point you to a very reliable source for it. If there's any truth to this notion of my supposed "wisdom"—if it *is* wisdom—then I will call upon the god of Delphi, Apollo, as my witness.

You all knew Chaerephon, I believe—[21a] a friend of mine since childhood, and a friend to your own democratic cause. He endured your exile and shared in your return to power.[7] You also know how he was—always getting carried away by some enthusiasm or another. So, he had the nerve to go off to Delphi one day—and please, don't interrupt—and ask the oracle: "Is anyone wiser than Socrates?" The priestess answered simply, "No one is wiser." Chaerephon is no longer with us, but his brother here will testify to these events.

Chaerephon's brother, Chaerecrates, steps forward to verify Socrates's statement.

[21b] σκέψασθε δὴ ὧν ἕνεκα ταῦτα λέγω· μέλλω γὰρ ὑμᾶς διδάξειν ὅθεν μοι ἡ διαβολὴ γέγονεν. ταῦτα γὰρ ἐγὼ ἀκούσας ἐνεθυμούμην οὑτωσί· "τί ποτε λέγει ὁ θεός, καὶ τί ποτε αἰνίττεται; ἐγὼ γὰρ δὴ οὔτε μέγα οὔτε σμικρὸν σύνοιδα ἐμαυτῷ σοφὸς ὤν· τί οὖν ποτε λέγει φάσκων ἐμὲ σοφώτατον εἶναι; οὐ γὰρ δήπου ψεύδεταί γε· οὐ γὰρ θέμις αὐτῷ."

καὶ πολὺν μὲν χρόνον ἠπόρουν τί ποτε λέγει· ἔπειτα μόγις πάνυ ἐπὶ ζήτησιν αὐτοῦ τοιαύτην τινὰ ἐτραπόμην. ἦλθον ἐπί τινα τῶν δοκούντων σοφῶν εἶναι, [21c] ὡς ἐνταῦθα εἴπερ που ἐλέγξων τὸ μαντεῖον καὶ ἀποφανῶν τῷ χρησμῷ ὅτι "οὑτοσὶ ἐμοῦ σοφώτερός ἐστι, σὺ δ᾽ ἐμὲ ἔφησθα." διασκοπῶν οὖν τοῦτον—ὀνόματι γὰρ οὐδὲν δέομαι λέγειν, ἦν δέ τις τῶν πολιτικῶν πρὸς ὃν ἐγὼ σκοπῶν τοιοῦτόν τι ἔπαθον, ὦ ἄνδρες Ἀθηναῖοι, καὶ διαλεγόμενος αὐτῷ—ἔδοξέ μοι οὗτος ὁ ἀνὴρ δοκεῖν μὲν εἶναι σοφὸς ἄλλοις τε πολλοῖς ἀνθρώποις καὶ μάλιστα ἑαυτῷ, εἶναι δ᾽ οὔ· κἄπειτα ἐπειρώμην αὐτῷ δεικνύναι ὅτι οἴοιτο

[21b] Now, think carefully about why I'm relating this story, because I'm about to explain the origin of the rumors about me. When I first heard it, see, I couldn't stop wondering: *What on earth does the god mean? What* is *this mystery?* I mean, I certainly don't feel especially—or even somewhat—wise. So what could he possibly mean in declaring me the *wisest*? He can't be lying, because that's not something gods can do.

For a long time, I couldn't grasp what the oracle was getting at. Then, quite reluctantly, I resolved to investigate. I decided the surest way to challenge the oracle's enigmatic claim was to visit someone reputed to be wise—because if [21c] it could be disproven, it would be there. I thought: *Now I can say: here is someone wiser than me, yet the oracle said* I *was.**

So, I went to a certain man—no need to name him, but he was a politician. And gentlemen, as I conversed with him, I couldn't shake the thought that although many believed him wise—and he believed it himself—he wasn't wise in the true sense at all. I tried to show him that while he thought

* Presumably meaning "... the oracle said *I* was the wisest," although the oracle did not quite say that, and Socrates does not quite say it here either.

μὲν εἶναι σοφός, [21d] εἴη δ' οὔ. ἐντεῦθεν οὖν τούτῳ τε ἀπηχθόμην καὶ πολλοῖς τῶν παρόντων· πρὸς ἐμαυτὸν δ' οὖν ἀπιὼν ἐλογιζόμην ὅτι

> τούτου μὲν τοῦ ἀνθρώπου ἐγὼ σοφώτερός εἰμι· κινδυνεύει μὲν γὰρ ἡμῶν οὐδέτερος οὐδὲν καλὸν κἀγαθὸν εἰδέναι, ἀλλ' οὗτος μὲν οἴεταί τι εἰδέναι οὐκ εἰδώς, ἐγὼ δέ, ὥσπερ οὖν οὐκ οἶδα, οὐδὲ οἴομαι· ἔοικα γοῦν τούτου γε σμικρῷ τινι αὐτῷ τούτῳ σοφώτερος εἶναι, ὅτι ἃ μὴ οἶδα οὐδὲ οἴομαι εἰδέναι.

ἐντεῦθεν ἐπ' ἄλλον ᾖα τῶν ἐκείνου δοκούντων σοφωτέρων εἶναι καί μοι ταὐτὰ ταῦτα ἔδοξε· [21e] καὶ ἐνταῦθα κἀκείνῳ καὶ ἄλλοις πολλοῖς ἀπηχθόμην.

μετὰ ταῦτ' οὖν ἤδη ἐφεξῆς ᾖα, αἰσθανόμενος μὲν καὶ λυπούμενος καὶ δεδιὼς ὅτι ἀπηχθανόμην, ὅμως δὲ ἀναγκαῖον ἐδόκει εἶναι τὸ τοῦ θεοῦ περὶ πλείστου ποιεῖσθαι· ἰτέον οὖν, σκοποῦντι τὸν χρησμὸν τί λέγει, [22a] ἐπὶ ἅπαντας τούς τι δοκοῦντας εἰδέναι. καὶ νὴ τὸν κύνα, ὦ ἄνδρες Ἀθηναῖοι—δεῖ γὰρ πρὸς ὑμᾶς τἀληθῆ λέγειν—ἦ μὴν ἐγὼ ἔπαθόν τι τοιοῦτον· οἱ μὲν

himself wise, [21d] he wasn't. Consequently, he and many others who were present took offense at me. As I left, I thought:

> *Well, compared to him, I must be wiser. Neither of us likely knows anything truly worthwhile, but this guy believes he does, though he doesn't. I, on the other hand, don't believe I know* anything—*and that, perhaps,* does *make me wiser by that modest measure: I don't know what I don't know, and I don't believe that I do.*

Next I went to another man—a man reputed to be wiser than the first—and it felt like the same story all over again. [21e] He too, along with many others, took offense and began to hate me.

After that I kept going, moving from one person to the next. I could see I was making enemies. I didn't like it, and it frightened me. Yet I felt I had no choice; I had to take the god's word seriously. I had to keep seeking the meaning of the oracle, [22a] visiting anyone who seemed likely to know something. And to be completely candid, I swear—because I must be truthful with you—that this was the result: as far as wisdom is concerned, those who

μάλιστα εὐδοκιμοῦντες ἔδοξάν μοι ὀλίγου δεῖν τοῦ πλείστου ἐνδεεῖς εἶναι ζητοῦντι κατὰ τὸν θεόν, ἄλλοι δὲ δοκοῦντες φαυλότεροι ἐπιεικέστεροι εἶναι ἄνδρες πρὸς τὸ φρονίμως ἔχειν.

δεῖ δὴ ὑμῖν τὴν ἐμὴν πλάνην ἐπιδεῖξαι ὥσπερ πόνους τινὰς πονοῦντος ἵνα μοι καὶ ἀνέλεγκτος ἡ μαντεία γένοιτο.

μετὰ γὰρ τοὺς πολιτικοὺς ᾖα ἐπὶ τοὺς ποιητὰς τούς τε τῶν τραγῳδιῶν καὶ [22b] τοὺς τῶν διθυράμβων καὶ τοὺς ἄλλους, ὡς ἐνταῦθα ἐπ' αὐτοφώρῳ καταληψόμενος ἐμαυτὸν ἀμαθέστερον ἐκείνων ὄντα. ἀναλαμβάνων οὖν αὐτῶν τὰ ποιήματα ἅ μοι ἐδόκει μάλιστα πεπραγματεῦσθαι αὐτοῖς, διηρώτων ἂν αὐτοὺς τί λέγοιεν, ἵν' ἅμα τι καὶ μανθάνοιμι παρ' αὐτῶν. αἰσχύνομαι οὖν ὑμῖν εἰπεῖν, ὦ ἄνδρες, τἀληθῆ· ὅμως δὲ ῥητέον. ὡς ἔπος γὰρ εἰπεῖν ὀλίγου αὐτῶν ἅπαντες οἱ παρόντες ἂν βέλτιον ἔλεγον περὶ ὧν αὐτοὶ ἐπεποιήκεσαν.

were the most highly regarded proved to be almost entirely lacking in it when I questioned them as the god commanded. Conversely, those regarded as less wise proved to be far more grounded in reality.

So, I must impress upon you how far I ventured and the herculean efforts I put into my quest—all to discover that the oracle's pronouncement was utterly irrefutable.*

After interviewing the politicians, see, I turned to the bards—the tragedians, [22b] choral lyricists, and so on—hoping I might prove that I'm less wise than they are. I studied the works they'd clearly poured their greatest effort into, and then questioned them about the meanings behind their texts. I hoped that by exposing my own ignorance, I might also learn something from them. And gentlemen, I must admit—it's embarrassing, but the truth must be told: virtually anybody there could have explained the meaning of those poems better than the bards themselves.

---

* Up until now, the translation "wise" for *sophia* has served well. To understand what follows, however, modern readers must know that the Greek word refers not only to deep understanding and moral insight, but also to skilled know-how in some practical domain, from writing songs to carving stone. Unfortunately, there is no single English word that captures both senses.

ἔγνων οὖν αὖ καὶ περὶ τῶν ποιητῶν ἐν ὀλίγῳ τοῦτο, ὅτι οὐ σοφίᾳ ποιοῖεν ἃ ποιοῖεν, [22c] ἀλλὰ φύσει τινὶ καὶ ἐνθουσιάζοντες ὥσπερ οἱ θεομάντεις καὶ οἱ χρησμῳδοί· καὶ γὰρ οὗτοι λέγουσι μὲν πολλὰ καὶ καλά, ἴσασιν δὲ οὐδὲν ὧν λέγουσι. τοιοῦτόν τί μοι ἐφάνησαν πάθος καὶ οἱ ποιηταὶ πεπονθότες, καὶ ἅμα ᾐσθόμην αὐτῶν διὰ τὴν ποίησιν οἰομένων καὶ τἆλλα σοφωτάτων εἶναι ἀνθρώπων ἃ οὐκ ἦσαν. ἀπῇα οὖν καὶ ἐντεῦθεν τῷ αὐτῷ οἰόμενος περιγεγονέναι ᾧπερ καὶ τῶν πολιτικῶν.

τελευτῶν οὖν ἐπὶ τοὺς χειροτέχνας ᾖα· [22d] ἐμαυτῷ γὰρ συνῄδη οὐδὲν ἐπισταμένῳ ὡς ἔπος εἰπεῖν, τούτους δέ γ᾽ ᾔδη ὅτι εὑρήσοιμι πολλὰ καὶ καλὰ ἐπισταμένους. καὶ τούτου μὲν οὐκ ἐψεύσθην, ἀλλ᾽ ἠπίσταντο ἃ ἐγὼ οὐκ ἠπιστάμην καί μου ταύτῃ σοφώτεροι ἦσαν. ἀλλ᾽, ὦ ἄνδρες Ἀθηναῖοι, ταὐτόν μοι ἔδοξαν ἔχειν ἁμάρτημα ὅπερ καὶ οἱ ποιηταὶ καὶ οἱ ἀγαθοὶ δημιουργοί—διὰ τὸ τὴν τέχνην καλῶς ἐξεργάζεσθαι ἕκαστος ἠξίου καὶ τἆλλα τὰ μέγιστα σοφώτατος εἶναι—καὶ αὐτῶν αὕτη ἡ πλημμέλεια ἐκείνην [22e] τὴν σοφίαν ἀποκρύπτειν·

So once again, in dealing with the bards, I learned a lesson. Their creations do not result from the application of wisdom or refined technique, [22c] but from some raw talent and a kind of divine inspiration or possession.[8] They resemble seers and soothsayers—uttering many impressive words without comprehending their own meaning. In my experience, the bards were in much that same position. At the same time, I noticed that because of their poetry, they fancied themselves the wisest about everything else as well—when, in reality, they were not. So I moved on again, believing that I was superior to them in precisely the same respect as I was to the politicians.

Finally, I went to those who work with their hands. [22d] I was well aware that I don't know much myself, but I was sure I'd find that at least these people knew many impressive things. And I wasn't wrong—they really did know things I didn't, and in that regard, they really were wiser than me. But, men of Athens, I noticed that our craftsmen shared the same fault as the bards: because each was so skilled in his one trade, he assumed he was the wisest about everything else, even really important issues. And that presumption overshadowed whatever wisdom he actually did have.[9] [22e] So I asked

ὥστε με ἐμαυτὸν ἀνερωτᾶν ὑπὲρ τοῦ χρησμοῦ πότερα δεξαίμην ἂν οὕτως ὥσπερ ἔχω ἔχειν, μήτε τι σοφὸς ὢν τὴν ἐκείνων σοφίαν μήτε ἀμαθὴς τὴν ἀμαθίαν, ἢ ἀμφότερα ἃ ἐκεῖνοι ἔχουσιν ἔχειν. ἀπεκρινάμην οὖν ἐμαυτῷ καὶ τῷ χρησμῷ ὅτι μοι λυσιτελοῖ ὥσπερ ἔχω ἔχειν.

ἐκ ταυτησὶ δὴ τῆς ἐξετάσεως, ὦ ἄνδρες Ἀθηναῖοι, [23a] πολλαὶ μὲν ἀπέχθειαί μοι γεγόνασι καὶ οἷαι χαλεπώταται καὶ βαρύταται, ὥστε πολλὰς διαβολὰς ἀπ᾽ αὐτῶν γεγονέναι, ὄνομα δὲ τοῦτο λέγεσθαι, σοφὸς εἶναι· οἴονται γάρ με ἑκάστοτε οἱ παρόντες ταῦτα αὐτὸν εἶναι σοφὸν ἃ ἂν ἄλλον ἐξελέγξω. τὸ δὲ κινδυνεύει, ὦ ἄνδρες, τῷ ὄντι ὁ θεὸς σοφὸς εἶναι, καὶ ἐν τῷ χρησμῷ τούτῳ τοῦτο λέγειν, ὅτι ἡ ἀνθρωπίνη σοφία ὀλίγου τινὸς ἀξία ἐστὶν καὶ οὐδενός. καὶ φαίνεται τοῦτον λέγειν τὸν Σωκράτη, προσκεχρῆσθαι δὲ τῷ ἐμῷ ὀνόματι, ἐμὲ παράδειγμα ποιούμενος, [23b] ὥσπερ ἂν <εἰ> εἴποι ὅτι "οὗτος ὑμῶν, ὦ ἄνθρωποι, σοφώτατός ἐστιν, ὅστις ὥσπερ Σωκράτης ἔγνωκεν ὅτι οὐδενὸς ἄξιός ἐστι τῇ ἀληθείᾳ πρὸς σοφίαν."

ταῦτ᾽ οὖν ἐγὼ μὲν ἔτι καὶ νῦν περιιὼν ζητῶ καὶ ἐρευνῶ κατὰ τὸν θεὸν καὶ τῶν ἀστῶν καὶ ξένων ἄν τινα οἴωμαι σοφὸν εἶναι· καὶ ἐπειδάν μοι μὴ δοκῇ, τῷ θεῷ βοηθῶν ἐνδείκνυμαι ὅτι οὐκ ἔστι σοφός. καὶ ὑπὸ ταύτης τῆς ἀσχολίας οὔτε τι τῶν τῆς πόλεως πρᾶξαί μοι σχολὴ γέγονεν ἄξιον λόγου οὔτε τῶν οἰκείων, ἀλλ᾽ ἐν πενίᾳ μυρίᾳ εἰμὶ διὰ τὴν τοῦ θεοῦ λατρείαν.

myself, as the oracle would have me, whether I'd rather be the way I am—not wise by their wisdom, and not foolish by their folly—or like them: knowledgeable in one field, but presumptuous enough to think I know it all. And I concluded—for both myself and the oracle—that I'm better off the way I am.

As a result of this inquiry, men of Athens, [23a] a great deal of resentment has grown up against me—resentment of the most bitter and difficult kind. With it have come many falsehoods, including this strange label, "wise." You see, whenever I ask a question about any topic, bystanders assume I must already be wise about it. But the truth is, gentlemen, it's the god who is truly wise. His oracle probably means that human wisdom is negligible, if it exists at all. And apparently, he's making an example of me—speaking through my name, and [23b] in effect declaring: "Humans, the wisest among you is he who, like Socrates, understands that when it comes to wisdom, he is nothing."

So that is why—even now—I traverse the city, searching and questioning anyone I have reason to believe is wise, whether citizen or foreigner, exactly as the god commands. And when these people appear unwise to me, I help the god out by showing them that they aren't. And because of this mission, I have no time for important matters, either of state

[23c] πρὸς δὲ τούτοις οἱ νέοι μοι <οἱ> ἐπακολουθοῦντες, οἷς μάλιστα σχολή ἐστιν, οἱ τῶν πλουσιωτάτων, αὐτόματοι, χαίρουσιν ἀκούοντες ἐξεταζομένων τῶν ἀνθρώπων, καὶ αὐτοὶ πολλάκις ἐμὲ μιμοῦνται, εἶτα ἐπιχειροῦσιν ἄλλους ἐξετάζειν· κἄπειτα οἶμαι εὑρίσκουσι πολλὴν ἀφθονίαν οἰομένων μὲν εἰδέναι τι ἀνθρώπων, εἰδότων δὲ ὀλίγα ἢ οὐδέν.

ἐντεῦθεν οὖν οἱ ὑπ᾽ αὐτῶν ἐξεταζόμενοι ἐμοὶ ὀργίζονται, [23d] οὐχ αὐτοῖς, καὶ λέγουσιν ὡς Σωκράτης τίς ἐστι μιαρώτατος καὶ διαφθείρει τοὺς νέους· καὶ ἐπειδάν τις αὐτοὺς ἐρωτᾷ ὅτι ποιῶν καὶ ὅτι διδάσκων, ἔχουσι μὲν οὐδὲν εἰπεῖν ἀλλ᾽ ἀγνοοῦσιν, ἵνα δὲ μὴ δοκῶσιν ἀπορεῖν, τὰ κατὰ πάντων τῶν φιλοσοφούντων πρόχειρα ταῦτα λέγουσιν, ὅτι “τὰ μετέωρα καὶ τὰ ὑπὸ γῆς” καὶ “θεοὺς μὴ νομίζειν” καὶ “τὸν ἥττω λόγον κρείττω ποιεῖν.” τὰ γὰρ ἀληθῆ οἴομαι οὐκ ἂν ἐθέλοιεν λέγειν, ὅτι κατάδηλοι γίγνονται προσποιούμενοι μὲν εἰδέναι, εἰδότες δὲ οὐδέν.

or in my personal affairs. As a result, I live in utter poverty—entirely by reason of my service to the god.

[23c] Add to all this that the young people who have taken to following me around—those with the most free time, the sons of the wealthiest—love listening to people being questioned. They often imitate me and start questioning others themselves. And I imagine they find plenty of people who think they know something, but in reality, know very little or nothing at all.

As a result, the people these young men examine get angry at *me*, [23d] not themselves, and start claiming that some man named Socrates is "poisoning their minds," that I'm "brainwashing the youth." When asked what I actually teach or do, they fall silent, because they have no answer. But instead of admitting they have no idea, they revert to the usual accusations leveled at freethinkers: that I speak about "things in the heavens and beneath the earth," that I "don't believe in the gods," and that I "make the weaker argument into the stronger one."[10] I doubt they'd ever admit the truth, because if they did they'd be exposed for what they really are: people pretending to know something, when in fact they know nothing.

[23e] ἅτε οὖν οἶμαι φιλότιμοι ὄντες καὶ σφοδροὶ καὶ πολλοί, καὶ συντεταμένως καὶ πιθανῶς λέγοντες περὶ ἐμοῦ, ἐμπεπλήκασιν ὑμῶν τὰ ὦτα καὶ πάλαι καὶ σφοδρῶς διαβάλλοντες. ἐκ τούτων καὶ Μέλητός μοι ἐπέθετο καὶ Ἄνυτος καὶ Λύκων, Μέλητος μὲν ὑπὲρ τῶν ποιητῶν ἀχθόμενος, Ἄνυτος δὲ ὑπὲρ τῶν δημιουργῶν καὶ τῶν πολιτικῶν, [24a] Λύκων δὲ ὑπὲρ τῶν ῥητόρων· ὥστε, ὅπερ ἀρχόμενος ἐγὼ ἔλεγον, θαυμάζοιμ' ἂν εἰ οἷός τ' εἴην ἐγὼ ὑμῶν ταύτην τὴν διαβολὴν ἐξελέσθαι ἐν οὕτως ὀλίγῳ χρόνῳ οὕτω πολλὴν γεγονυῖαν.

ταῦτ' ἔστιν ὑμῖν, ὦ ἄνδρες Ἀθηναῖοι, τἀληθῆ, καὶ ὑμᾶς οὔτε μέγα οὔτε μικρὸν ἀποκρυψάμενος ἐγὼ λέγω οὐδ' ὑποστειλάμενος. καίτοι οἶδα σχεδὸν ὅτι αὐτοῖς τούτοις ἀπεχθάνομαι, ὃ καὶ τεκμήριον ὅτι ἀληθῆ λέγω καὶ ὅτι αὕτη ἐστὶν ἡ διαβολὴ ἡ ἐμὴ καὶ τὰ αἴτια ταῦτά ἐστιν. [24b] καὶ ἐάντε νῦν ἐάντε αὖθις ζητήσητε ταῦτα, οὕτως εὑρήσετε.

περὶ μὲν οὖν ὧν οἱ πρῶτοί μου κατήγοροι κατηγόρουν αὕτη ἔστω ἱκανὴ ἀπολογία πρὸς ὑμᾶς· πρὸς δὲ Μέλητον τὸν ἀγαθὸν καὶ φιλόπολιν, ὥς φησι, καὶ τοὺς ὑστέρους μετὰ ταῦτα πειράσομαι ἀπολογήσασθαι. αὖθις γὰρ δή, ὥσπερ ἑτέρων τούτων ὄντων κατηγόρων, λάβωμεν αὖ τὴν τούτων ἀντωμοσίαν. ἔχει δέ πως ὧδε·

[23e] In my view, it's because these people—vain, relentless, and numerous—speak of me with such compelling force that they filled your ears long ago with their fervent demonizations. Among them, Meletus attacked me, while Anytus and Lycon joined in—Meletus looking for revenge on behalf of the bards, Anytus for the craftsmen and politicians, and [24a] Lycon representing the orators. As I said at the outset, it would be a miracle if I could dispel this prejudice in the short time we have, considering how deeply it has taken root.

And that, men of Athens, is the truth. I've told you everything, without hiding or holding anything back, no matter how big or small. And yet, I am just about certain that these people do hate me, and for these reasons, which only proves I'm telling the truth. This is the slander against me, and this is its root cause. [24b] If you investigate these matters, either now or at a future time, you will find them to be true.[11]

Gentlemen, let this suffice as a response to the accusations brought against me by my first accusers. Now I'll try to address the charges brought by Meletus, the "good, patriotic" man, as he calls himself, and the more recent accusers. Once more, as if these were new charges, let us examine their complaint. It goes roughly like this:

Σωκράτη φησὶν ἀδικεῖν τούς τε νέους διαφθείροντα καὶ θεοὺς οὓς ἡ πόλις [24c] νομίζει οὐ νομίζοντα, ἕτερα δὲ δαιμόνια καινά.

τὸ μὲν δὴ ἔγκλημα τοιοῦτόν ἐστιν· τούτου δὲ τοῦ ἐγκλήματος ἓν ἕκαστον ἐξετάσωμεν.

φησὶ γὰρ δὴ τοὺς νέους ἀδικεῖν με διαφθείροντα. ἐγὼ δέ γε, ὦ ἄνδρες Ἀθηναῖοι, ἀδικεῖν φημι Μέλητον, ὅτι σπουδῇ χαριεντίζεται, ῥᾳδίως εἰς ἀγῶνα καθιστὰς ἀνθρώπους, περὶ πραγμάτων προσποιούμενος σπουδάζειν καὶ κήδεσθαι ὧν οὐδὲν τούτῳ πώποτε ἐμέλησεν· ὡς δὲ τοῦτο οὕτως ἔχει, πειράσομαι καὶ ὑμῖν ἐπιδεῖξαι.

καί μοι δεῦρο, ὦ Μέλητε, εἰπέ·

ΣΩΚΡΑΤΗΣ: ἄλλο τι ἢ περὶ πλείστου [24d] ποιῇ ὅπως ὡς βέλτιστοι οἱ νεώτεροι ἔσονται;

ΜΕΛΗΤΟΣ: ἔγωγε.

ΣΩΚΡΑΤΗΣ: ἴθι δή νυν εἰπὲ τούτοις, τίς αὐτοὺς βελτίους ποιεῖ; δῆλον γὰρ ὅτι οἶσθα, μέλον γέ σοι. τὸν μὲν γὰρ διαφθείροντα ἐξευρών, ὡς φῄς,

> Socrates is guilty of brainwashing the youth and not believing in the gods the city [24c] believes in, but in different, new idols instead.[12]

That's more or less it, but let's break it down and look at each part closely.

Meletus claims I'm guilty of brainwashing the youth. But I, gentlemen, hold that it's *Meletus* who is guilty—guilty of flippant nonchalance, of dragging men into court frivolously, and of posing as a guardian of serious issues while feigning "meticulous" care for matters he never really cared about.

Let me now try to show you why that's true. Come up here, Meletus, and tell me—

Meletus steps forward.

SOCRATES: Isn't it true you believe it's of the utmost importance [24d] that the younger generation live up to its potential?

MELETUS: I do.

SOCRATES: Alright, now tell me—who is responsible for *making* them live up to their potential? Clearly you know, since it's something you show meticulous care for. Because, you see, now that you've found the man who's

ἐμέ, εἰσάγεις τουτοισὶ καὶ κατηγορεῖς· τὸν δὲ δὴ βελτίους ποιοῦντα ἴθι εἰπὲ καὶ μήνυσον αὐτοῖς τίς ἐστιν.

ὁρᾷς, ὦ Μέλητε, ὅτι σιγᾷς καὶ οὐκ ἔχεις εἰπεῖν; καίτοι οὐκ αἰσχρόν σοι δοκεῖ εἶναι καὶ ἱκανὸν τεκμήριον οὗ δὴ ἐγὼ λέγω, ὅτι σοι οὐδὲν μεμέληκεν; ἀλλ᾽ εἰπέ, ὠγαθέ, τίς αὐτοὺς ἀμείνους ποιεῖ;

ΜΕΛΗΤΟΣ: οἱ νόμοι.

ΣΩΚΡΑΤΗΣ [24e]: ἀλλ᾽ οὐ τοῦτο ἐρωτῶ, ὦ βέλτιστε, ἀλλὰ τίς ἄνθρωπος, ὅστις πρῶτον καὶ αὐτὸ τοῦτο οἶδε, τοὺς νόμους;

ΜΕΛΗΤΟΣ: οὗτοι, ὦ Σώκρατες, οἱ δικασταί.

ΣΩΚΡΑΤΗΣ: πῶς λέγεις, ὦ Μέλητε; οἵδε τοὺς νέους παιδεύειν οἷοί τέ εἰσι καὶ βελτίους ποιοῦσιν;

ΜΕΛΗΤΟΣ: μάλιστα.

ΣΩΚΡΑΤΗΣ: πότερον ἅπαντες, ἢ οἱ μὲν αὐτῶν, οἱ δ᾽ οὔ;

ΜΕΛΗΤΟΣ: ἅπαντες.

supposedly brainwashing the youth—me, that is—you've brought me to court and accused me of these crimes. But who actually makes them live up to their *potential*? Come on, tell us who it is.

Meletus says nothing.

Do you see, Meletus, that you're staying quiet and can't answer? Don't you think that's embarrassing, and proof of what I've been saying—that you show no meticulous care for the issue at all? So come on, my fine friend, tell us. Who makes them *better*?

MELETUS: The laws.

SOCRATES [24e]: But that's not what I'm asking, my good sir. I'm asking, who is the *person* that actually knows the laws in the first place, and so makes them better?

MELETUS: These men here, Socrates, the jurors.

SOCRATES: Wait a second, Meletus. You're saying these men are able to teach the youth and make them live up to their potential?

MELETUS: Absolutely.

SOCRATES: All of them, or just some of them?

MELETUS: All of them.

ΣΩΚΡΑΤΗΣ: εὖγε νὴ τὴν Ἥραν λέγεις καὶ πολλὴν ἀφθονίαν τῶν ὠφελούντων. τί δὲ δή; οἱ δὲ ἀκροαταὶ βελτίους ποιοῦσιν ἢ οὔ;

ΜΕΛΗΤΟΣ [25a]: καὶ οὗτοι.

ΣΩΚΡΑΤΗΣ: τί δέ, οἱ βουλευταί;

ΜΕΛΗΤΟΣ: καὶ οἱ βουλευταί.

ΣΩΚΡΑΤΗΣ: ἀλλ' ἄρα, ὦ Μέλητε, μὴ οἱ ἐν τῇ ἐκκλησίᾳ, οἱ ἐκκλησιασταί, διαφθείρουσι τοὺς νεωτέρους; ἢ κἀκεῖνοι βελτίους ποιοῦσιν ἅπαντες;

ΜΕΛΗΤΟΣ: κἀκεῖνοι.

ΣΩΚΡΑΤΗΣ: πάντες ἄρα, ὡς ἔοικεν, Ἀθηναῖοι καλοὺς κἀγαθοὺς ποιοῦσι πλὴν ἐμοῦ, ἐγὼ δὲ μόνος διαφθείρω. οὕτω λέγεις;

ΜΕΛΗΤΟΣ: πάνυ σφόδρα ταῦτα λέγω.

ΣΩΚΡΑΤΗΣ: πολλήν γέ μου κατέγνωκας δυστυχίαν. καί μοι ἀπόκριναι· ἦ καὶ περὶ ἵππους οὕτω σοι δοκεῖ ἔχειν; [25b] οἱ μὲν βελτίους ποιοῦντες αὐτοὺς πάντες ἄνθρωποι εἶναι, εἷς δέ τις ὁ διαφθείρων; ἢ τοὐναντίον τούτου πᾶν

SOCRATES: Bravo, *bravo!* You've identified quite a lot of people who benefit them! But hang on—what about the audience here observing us? Do they make the youth live up to their potential, or not?

MELETUS [25a]: They do too.

SOCRATES: And what about the Council members?

MELETUS: The Council members do too.

SOCRATES: And surely, Meletus, those in the Assembly, the Assemblymen—they don't brainwash the youth, do they? Or do all of them make the youth live up to their potential as well?

MELETUS: They do too.

SOCRATES: So everyone in Athens, it seems, produces fine, upstanding gentlemen—except for me. I alone brainwash them. This is what you're saying?

MELETUS: You better believe that's what I'm saying.

SOCRATES: What a miserable fate you've consigned me to! But okay, answer me this: do you think the same applies to horses? [25b] Is it true that all people make them live up to their potential, while only one person "brainwashes" them? Isn't it totally the opposite? That one

εἷς μέν τις ὁ βελτίους οἷός τ᾽ ὢν ποιεῖν ἢ πάνυ ὀλίγοι, οἱ ἱππικοί, οἱ δὲ πολλοὶ ἐάνπερ συνῶσι καὶ χρῶνται ἵπποις, διαφθείρουσιν; οὐχ οὕτως ἔχει, ὦ Μέλητε, καὶ περὶ ἵππων καὶ τῶν ἄλλων ἁπάντων ζῴων;

πάντως δήπου, ἐάντε σὺ καὶ Ἄνυτος οὐ φῆτε ἐάντε φῆτε· πολλὴ γὰρ ἄν τις εὐδαιμονία εἴη περὶ τοὺς νέους εἰ εἷς μὲν μόνος αὐτοὺς διαφθείρει, οἱ δ᾽ ἄλλοι ὠφελοῦσιν. [25c] ἀλλὰ γάρ, ὦ Μέλητε, ἱκανῶς ἐπιδείκνυσαι ὅτι οὐδεπώποτε ἐφρόντισας τῶν νέων, καὶ σαφῶς ἀποφαίνεις τὴν σαυτοῦ ἀμέλειαν, ὅτι οὐδέν σοι μεμέληκεν περὶ ὧν ἐμὲ εἰσάγεις.

ἔτι δὲ ἡμῖν εἰπέ, ὦ πρὸς Διὸς Μέλητε, πότερόν ἐστιν οἰκεῖν ἄμεινον ἐν πολίταις χρηστοῖς ἢ πονηροῖς; ὦ τάν, ἀπόκριναι· οὐδὲν γάρ τοι χαλεπὸν ἐρωτῶ. οὐχ οἱ μὲν πονηροὶ κακόν τι ἐργάζονται τοὺς ἀεὶ ἐγγυτάτω αὑτῶν ὄντας, οἱ δ᾽ ἀγαθοὶ ἀγαθόν τι;

ΜΕΛΗΤΟΣ: πάνυ γε.

person, or just a very few who are skilled in horse training, are able to make them live up to their potential, while the majority, if they handle or use horses, "brainwash" them? Isn't that how it works, Meletus, with horses and every other animal?

Meletus says nothing.

Of course it is, whether you and Anytus admit it or not. It would truly be a blessing for our youth if only a single person brainwashed them while everyone else helped them. [25c] The truth is, Meletus, you're showing all too clearly that you're not "meticulous." You've never really given any thought to young people. You've made your uncaring attitude manifest, and it's clear that you don't really care—meticulously or otherwise—about the matters you've brought against me.

Now for the love of God, Meletus, tell us this—which is better: living among good citizens, or bad ones? Answer, sir; it's not a hard question. Don't bad people do bad to whoever is around them, while good people do good?

MELETUS: Of course.

ΣΩΚΡΑΤΗΣ [25d]: ἔστιν οὖν ὅστις βούλεται ὑπὸ τῶν συνόντων βλάπτεσθαι μᾶλλον ἢ ὠφελεῖσθαι; ἀποκρίνου, ὦ ἀγαθέ· καὶ γὰρ ὁ νόμος κελεύει ἀποκρίνεσθαι. ἔσθ' ὅστις βούλεται βλάπτεσθαι;|

ΜΕΛΗΤΟΣ: οὐ δῆτα.

ΣΩΚΡΑΤΗΣ: φέρε δή, πότερον ἐμὲ εἰσάγεις δεῦρο ὡς διαφθείροντα τοὺς νέους καὶ πονηροτέρους ποιοῦντα ἑκόντα ἢ ἄκοντα;

ΜΕΛΗΤΟΣ: ἑκόντα ἔγωγε.

ΣΩΚΡΑΤΗΣ: τί δῆτα, ὦ Μέλητε; τοσοῦτον σὺ ἐμοῦ σοφώτερος εἶ τηλικούτου ὄντος τηλικόσδε ὤν, ὥστε σὺ μὲν ἔγνωκας ὅτι οἱ μὲν κακοὶ κακόν τι ἐργάζονται ἀεὶ τοὺς μάλιστα πλησίον ἑαυτῶν, οἱ δὲ ἀγαθοὶ ἀγαθόν, [25e] ἐγὼ δὲ δὴ εἰς τοσοῦτον ἀμαθίας ἥκω ὥστε καὶ τοῦτ' ἀγνοῶ, ὅτι ἐάν τινα μοχθηρὸν ποιήσω τῶν συνόντων, κινδυνεύσω κακόν τι λαβεῖν ὑπ' αὐτοῦ, ὥστε τοῦτο <τὸ> τοσοῦτον κακὸν ἑκὼν ποιῶ, ὡς φῄς σύ;

ταῦτα ἐγώ σοι οὐ πείθομαι, ὦ Μέλητε, οἶμαι δὲ οὐδὲ ἄλλον ἀνθρώπων οὐδένα· ἀλλ' ἢ οὐ διαφθείρω ἤ, [26a] εἰ διαφθείρω, ἄκων, ὥστε σύ γε κατ' ἀμφότερα ψεύδῃ. εἰ δὲ ἄκων διαφθείρω, τῶν τοιούτων ἁμαρτημάτων οὐ δεῦρο νόμος

SOCRATES [25d]: Alright then, is there anyone who actually wants to be harmed by the people they associate with instead of helped? Answer me, my good man—the law says you have to. Does *anyone* want to be harmed?

MELETUS: Of course not.

SOCRATES: Okay then, are you charging me with brainwashing the youth and making them worse on purpose, or by accident?

MELETUS: On purpose, I tell you.

SOCRATES: Really, Meletus? You're saying you're so much wiser than me, despite being so much younger, that you understand this simple fact—that bad people always do bad to those closest to them, while good people do them good [25e]—yet *I* am so utterly stupid that I don't even realize that if I taint and corrupt someone close to me, I'll risk getting harmed by him in return? That I'd do something so bad on purpose, as you say?

I don't believe you, Meletus, and I doubt anyone else does either. The truth is, I'm either not brainwashing the youth, or if [26a] I am, I'm doing it unintentionally. Either way, your charge against me is false. If I'm doing it unintentionally, the law doesn't call for dragging me here to court for such mistakes. You're supposed

εἰσάγειν ἐστίν, ἀλλὰ ἰδίᾳ λαβόντα διδάσκειν καὶ νουθετεῖν· δῆλον γὰρ ὅτι ἐὰν μάθω, παύσομαι ὅ γε ἄκων ποιῶ. σὺ δὲ συγγενέσθαι μέν μοι καὶ διδάξαι ἔφυγες καὶ οὐκ ἠθέλησας, δεῦρο δὲ εἰσάγεις, οἷ νόμος ἐστὶν εἰσάγειν τοὺς κολάσεως δεομένους ἀλλ᾽ οὐ μαθήσεως.

ἀλλὰ γάρ, ὦ ἄνδρες Ἀθηναῖοι, τοῦτο μὲν δῆλον ἤδη ἐστίν οὑγὼ ἔλεγον, [26b] ὅτι Μελήτῳ τούτων οὔτε μέγα οὔτε μικρὸν πώποτε ἐμέλησεν. ὅμως δὲ δὴ λέγε ἡμῖν, πῶς με φῂς διαφθείρειν, ὦ Μέλητε, τοὺς νεωτέρους; ἢ δῆλον δὴ ὅτι κατὰ τὴν γραφὴν ἣν ἐγράψω θεοὺς διδάσκοντα μὴ νομίζειν οὓς ἡ πόλις νομίζει, ἕτερα δὲ δαιμόνια καινά; οὐ ταῦτα λέγεις ὅτι διδάσκων διαφθείρω;

ΜΕΛΗΤΟΣ: πάνυ μὲν οὖν σφόδρα ταῦτα λέγω.

ΣΩΚΡΑΤΗΣ: πρὸς αὐτῶν τοίνυν, ὦ Μέλητε, τούτων τῶν θεῶν ὧν νῦν ὁ λόγος ἐστίν, εἰπὲ ἔτι σαφέστερον καὶ ἐμοὶ καὶ τοῖς ἀνδράσιν τουτοισί. [26c] ἐγὼ γὰρ οὐ δύναμαι μαθεῖν πότερον λέγεις διδάσκειν με νομίζειν εἶναί τινας θεούς—καὶ αὐτὸς ἄρα νομίζω εἶναι θεοὺς καὶ οὐκ εἰμὶ τὸ

to take me aside privately instead, and teach me, and set me straight. Because if I'm told about it, I'll obviously stop doing what I'm doing unintentionally. But you avoided getting to know me and teaching me; you weren't willing to. Instead, you've dragged me here to court, where the law only deals with people who need punishment, not education.

But really, men of Athens, this much is already clear from what I've said: [26b] Meletus has never cared, meticulously or otherwise, about these things. Still, tell us, Meletus, exactly how, in your view, I brainwash the youth. Is it by doing what that complaint you filed says—teaching them "not to believe in the gods the city believes in, but different, new idols instead"? Isn't that what you're saying—that I brainwash them by teaching that?

MELETUS: You better believe it. That's exactly what I'm saying.

SOCRATES: Alright then, Meletus, in the name of the very gods we're now talking about, let's hear it straight from you. Be even clearer with me and these men here. [26c] I can't tell whether you're accusing me of teaching people to believe that *some* gods exist—meaning that I myself believe that gods exist, so that I'm not

παράπαν ἄθεος οὐδὲ ταύτῃ ἀδικῶ—οὐ μέντοι οὔσπερ γε ἡ πόλις ἀλλὰ ἑτέρους, καὶ τοῦτ᾽ ἔστιν ὅ μοι ἐγκαλεῖς, ὅτι ἑτέρους, ἢ παντάπασί με φῂς οὔτε αὐτὸν νομίζειν θεοὺς τούς τε ἄλλους ταῦτα διδάσκειν.

ΜΕΛΗΤΟΣ: ταῦτα λέγω, ὡς τὸ παράπαν οὐ νομίζεις θεούς.

ΣΩΚΡΑΤΗΣ [26d]: ὦ θαυμάσιε Μέλητε, ἵνα τί ταῦτα λέγεις; οὐδὲ ἥλιον οὐδὲ σελήνην ἄρα νομίζω θεοὺς εἶναι, ὥσπερ οἱ ἄλλοι ἄνθρωποι;

ΜΕΛΗΤΟΣ: μὰ Δί᾽, ὦ ἄνδρες δικασταί, ἐπεὶ τὸν μὲν ἥλιον λίθον φησὶν εἶναι, τὴν δὲ σελήνην γῆν.

ΣΩΚΡΑΤΗΣ: Ἀναξαγόρου οἴει κατηγορεῖν, ὦ φίλε Μέλητε; καὶ οὕτω καταφρονεῖς τῶνδε καὶ οἴει αὐτοὺς ἀπείρους γραμμάτων εἶναι ὥστε οὐκ εἰδέναι ὅτι τὰ Ἀναξαγόρου βιβλία τοῦ Κλαζομενίου γέμει τούτων τῶν λόγων; καὶ δὴ καὶ οἱ νέοι ταῦτα παρ᾽ ἐμοῦ μανθάνουσιν, ἃ ἔξεστιν ἐνίοτε εἰ πάνυ [26e] πολλοῦ δραχμῆς ἐκ τῆς ὀρχήστρας πριαμένοις Σωκράτους καταγελᾶν, ἐὰν προσποιῆται ἑαυτοῦ εἶναι, ἄλλως τε καὶ οὕτως ἄτοπα ὄντα; ἀλλ᾽, ὦ πρὸς Διός, οὑτωσί σοι

a total atheist and guilty of that charge—just not the gods the city believes in, but other gods instead, and that's what you're charging me with? Or are you claiming that I don't believe in gods at all myself and teach others the same?

MELETUS: That is what I'm saying: you don't believe in any gods whatsoever.

SOCRATES [26d]: Meletus, you really are something else. Why would you say that? Are you claiming I don't even believe the sun and the moon are gods, like everyone else does?

MELETUS: For the love of god, gentlemen of the jury, that's precisely what I'm saying! He says the sun is a stone and the moon is made of earth.

SOCRATES: My dear Meletus, do you think it's Anaxagoras you're putting on trial? Do you really think so little of these jurors, do you imagine them so illiterate that they don't know the books of Anaxagoras of Clazomenae are full of ideas like that? Are you seriously suggesting the young pick up these notions from me—ideas they can [26e] buy for a drachma or less in the marketplace, and then ridicule Socrates for claiming them as his own? Especially when they're so odd? Come on. Is that what

δοκῶ; οὐδένα νομίζω θεὸν εἶναι;

ΜΕΛΗΤΟΣ: οὐ μέντοι μὰ Δία οὐδ᾽ ὁπωστιοῦν.
ΣΩΚΡΑΤΗΣ: ἄπιστός γ᾽ εἶ, ὦ Μέλητε, καὶ ταῦτα μέντοι, ὡς ἐμοὶ δοκεῖς, σαυτῷ. ἐμοὶ γὰρ δοκεῖ οὑτοσί, ὦ ἄνδρες Ἀθηναῖοι, πάνυ εἶναι ὑβριστὴς καὶ ἀκόλαστος, καὶ ἀτεχνῶς τὴν γραφὴν ταύτην ὕβρει τινὶ καὶ ἀκολασίᾳ καὶ νεότητι γράψασθαι. [27a] ἔοικεν γὰρ ὥσπερ αἴνιγμα συντιθέντι διαπειρωμένῳ "ἆρα γνώσεται Σωκράτης ὁ σοφὸς δὴ ἐμοῦ χαριεντιζομένου καὶ ἐναντί᾽ ἐμαυτῷ λέγοντος, ἢ ἐξαπατήσω αὐτὸν καὶ τοὺς ἄλλους τοὺς ἀκούοντας;" οὗτος γὰρ ἐμοὶ φαίνεται τὰ ἐναντία λέγειν αὐτὸς ἑαυτῷ ἐν τῇ γραφῇ ὥσπερ ἂν εἰ εἴποι· "ἀδικεῖ Σωκράτης θεοὺς οὐ νομίζων, ἀλλὰ θεοὺς νομίζων." καίτοι τοῦτό ἐστι παίζοντος.

συνεπισκέψασθε δή, ὦ ἄνδρες, ᾗ μοι φαίνεται ταῦτα λέγειν· σὺ δὲ ἡμῖν ἀπόκριναι, ὦ Μέλητε. [27b] ὑμεῖς δέ, ὅπερ κατ᾽ ἀρχὰς ὑμᾶς παρῃτησάμην, μέμνησθέ μοι μὴ θορυβεῖν ἐὰν ἐν τῷ εἰωθότι τρόπῳ τοὺς λόγους ποιῶμαι.

ἔστιν ὅστις ἀνθρώπων, ὦ Μέλητε, ἀνθρώπεια μὲν νομίζει πράγματ᾽ εἶναι, ἀνθρώπους δὲ οὐ νομίζει;

you really think of me? That I don't believe in the existence of any god at all?[13]

MELETUS: Exactly. Not a single one at all!

SOCRATES: Meletus, you really are unbelievable. And honestly, I'm not even sure you believe yourself. It looks to me, men of Athens, like this man is absolutely arrogant and reckless. All he did was file this complaint as some kind of arrogant, reckless, immature stunt. [27a] It's like he's playing a little riddle game: "Is 'wise old Socrates' going to spot my joke—that I'm contradicting myself—or will I fool him and everybody else listening?" I mean, it looks to me as if he's contradicting himself in the complaint itself. It's like saying, "Socrates is guilty of not believing in gods, but also of believing in gods." This is what children do for fun.

So take a closer look with me, gentlemen, at why it seems to me that this is precisely what he's suggesting. And you, Meletus, answer us. [27b] As for the rest of you, remember what I said at the start, and let's not have any angry outburst from you if I make my arguments in my customary manner.

Tell me, Meletus: is there any human who believes in the existence of human activities but doesn't believe in human beings?

ἀποκρινέσθω, ὦ ἄνδρες, καὶ μὴ ἄλλα καὶ ἄλλα θορυβείτω· ἔσθ᾽ ὅστις ἵππους μὲν οὐ νομίζει, ἱππικὰ δὲ πράγματα; ἢ αὐλητὰς μὲν οὐ νομίζει εἶναι, αὐλητικὰ δὲ πράγματα;

οὐκ ἔστιν, ὦ ἄριστε ἀνδρῶν· εἰ μὴ σὺ βούλει ἀποκρίνεσθαι, ἐγὼ σοὶ λέγω καὶ τοῖς ἄλλοις τουτοισί. ἀλλὰ τὸ ἐπὶ τούτῳ γε ἀπόκριναι· ἔσθ᾽ ὅστις δαιμόνια μὲν νομίζει πράγματ᾽ εἶναι, [27c] δαίμονας δὲ οὐ νομίζει;

ΜΕΛΗΤΟΣ: οὐκ ἔστιν.

ΣΩΚΡΑΤΗΣ: ὡς ὤνησας ὅτι μόγις ἀπεκρίνω ὑπὸ τουτωνὶ ἀναγκαζόμενος. οὐκοῦν δαιμόνια μὲν φῂς με καὶ νομίζειν καὶ διδάσκειν, εἴτ᾽ οὖν καινὰ εἴτε παλαιά, ἀλλ᾽ οὖν δαιμόνιά γε νομίζω κατὰ τὸν σὸν λόγον, καὶ ταῦτα καὶ διωμόσω ἐν τῇ

Meletus glares and blows a raspberry.

Make him answer the question, gentlemen, and don't let him just keep jeering. Is there anyone who doesn't believe in horses but does believe in horse activities? Or doesn't believe in the existence of musicians but does believe in playing music as an activity?

Meletus sulks in silence.

There isn't, my fine fellow. If you don't want to answer, let me say it for you and everyone else here. But at least answer me this next one: is there anyone who believes in the existence of angelic activities [27c] but doesn't believe in angels?

Meletus continues to sulk until some jurors shout at him to answer the question.

MELETUS: No, there isn't.

SOCRATES: How kind of you to answer—albeit reluctantly, and under compulsion from these folks here. Okay: you say I believe in and teach about angelic activities, whether new or old. By your own account, then, I do believe

ἀντιγραφῇ. εἰ δὲ δαιμόνια νομίζω, καὶ δαίμονας δήπου πολλὴ ἀνάγκη νομίζειν μέ ἐστιν· οὐχ οὕτως ἔχει;

ἔχει δή· τίθημι γάρ σε ὁμολογοῦντα, ἐπειδὴ οὐκ ἀποκρίνῃ. [27d] τοὺς δὲ δαίμονας οὐχὶ ἤτοι θεούς γε ἡγούμεθα ἢ θεῶν παῖδας; φῂς ἢ οὔ;

ΜΕΛΗΤΟΣ: πάνυ γε.

ΣΩΚΡΑΤΗΣ: οὐκοῦν εἴπερ δαίμονας ἡγοῦμαι, ὡς σὺ φῄς, εἰ μὲν θεοί τινές εἰσιν οἱ δαίμονες, τοῦτ᾽ ἂν εἴη ὃ ἐγώ φημί σε αἰνίττεσθαι καὶ χαριεντίζεσθαι, θεοὺς οὐχ ἡγούμενον φάναι με θεοὺς αὖ ἡγεῖσθαι πάλιν, ἐπειδήπερ γε δαίμονας ἡγοῦμαι· εἰ δ᾽ αὖ οἱ δαίμονες θεῶν παῖδές εἰσιν νόθοι τινὲς ἢ ἐκ νυμφῶν ἢ ἔκ τινων ἄλλων ὧν δὴ καὶ λέγονται, τίς ἂν ἀνθρώπων θεῶν μὲν παῖδας ἡγοῖτο εἶναι, θεοὺς δὲ μή; [27e] ὁμοίως γὰρ ἂν ἄτοπον εἴη ὥσπερ ἂν εἴ τις ἵππων μὲν παῖδας

in angelic activities. You even affirmed this in the complaint. Now, if I believe in angelic activities, then doesn't it follow—completely automatically—that I believe in angels too? Isn't that the logical conclusion?

Meletus sulks in silence.

It is—I mean, I take it you agree, since you didn't answer. [27d] And angels—don't we consider them actual gods, or else children of gods? Yes or no?

MELETUS: Of course.

SOCRATES: So, if I believe in angels, as you say—and if these angels are, in some sense, gods of a sort—then that is why I say you're playing some kind of riddle game. You charge me with not believing in gods while simultaneously asserting I do believe in gods, since I accept the existence of angels. Now, follow me here: if these angels are the illegitimate offspring of gods, born from nymphs, say, or other such beings as we're told they are, then who could believe in the children of gods without believing in the gods themselves? [27e] That's as bizarre as believing in mules—the offspring of

ἡγοῖτο καὶ ὄνων, τοὺς ἡμιόνους, ἵππους δὲ καὶ ὄνους μὴ ἡγοῖτο εἶναι.

ἀλλ᾽, ὦ Μέλητε, οὐκ ἔστιν ὅπως σὺ ταῦτα οὐχὶ ἀποπειρώμενος ἡμῶν ἐγράψω τὴν γραφὴν ταύτην ἢ ἀπορῶν ὅτι ἐγκαλοῖς ἐμοὶ ἀληθὲς ἀδίκημα· ὅπως δὲ σύ τινα πείθοις ἂν καὶ σμικρὸν νοῦν ἔχοντα ἀνθρώπων, ὡς τοῦ αὐτοῦ ἔστιν καὶ δαιμόνια καὶ θεῖα ἡγεῖσθαι, [28a] καὶ αὖ τοῦ αὐτοῦ μήτε δαίμονας μήτε θεοὺς μήτε ἥρωας, οὐδεμία μηχανή ἐστιν.

ἀλλὰ γάρ, ὦ ἄνδρες Ἀθηναῖοι, ὡς μὲν ἐγὼ οὐκ ἀδικῶ κατὰ τὴν Μελήτου γραφήν, οὐ πολλῆς μοι δοκεῖ εἶναι ἀπολογίας, ἀλλὰ ἱκανὰ καὶ ταῦτα· ὃ δὲ καὶ ἐν τοῖς ἔμπροσθεν ἔλεγον, ὅτι πολλή μοι ἀπέχθεια γέγονεν καὶ πρὸς πολλούς, εὖ ἴστε ὅτι ἀληθές ἐστιν. καὶ τοῦτ᾽ ἔστιν ὃ ἐμὲ αἱρήσει, ἐάνπερ αἱρῇ, οὐ Μέλητος οὐδὲ Ἄνυτος ἀλλ᾽ ἡ τῶν πολλῶν διαβολή τε καὶ φθόνος. ἃ δὴ πολλοὺς καὶ ἄλλους καὶ [28b] ἀγαθοὺς ἄνδρας ᾕρηκεν, οἶμαι δὲ καὶ αἱρήσει· οὐδὲν δὲ δεινὸν μὴ ἐν ἐμοὶ στῇ.

ἴσως ἂν οὖν εἴποι τις·

“εἶτ᾽ οὐκ αἰσχύνῃ, ὦ Σώκρατες, τοιοῦτον ἐπιτήδευμα ἐπιτηδεύσας ἐξ οὗ κινδυνεύεις νυνὶ ἀποθανεῖν;”

> horses and donkeys—while denying that horses and donkeys exist.[14]

Well, Meletus, there's no way you brought this case in earnest—either this is a joke, or you simply had nothing real to charge me with. But how could you possibly convince anyone with even a shred of sense that the same person might believe in the activities of angels and gods, [28a] and yet somehow not in angels or gods or saints? It doesn't add up.

Anyway, men of Athens, I don't believe a long speech is necessary to prove I'm not guilty of Meletus's charges; what I've already said should suffice. But as I stated earlier, a deep-seated resentment and envy have taken hold in many people—you must understand, *that* part is true. And that will be the cause of my downfall today, if down I do go. It won't be because of Meletus or Anytus—it will be because of that widespread prejudice and envy. It's already brought down many [28b] good men before me, and I fear it will continue to do so. There's no reason to think it will stop with me.

Perhaps someone might say:

> "Socrates, aren't you ashamed of choosing a way of life that now places you at risk of being put to death?"

ἐγὼ δὲ τούτῳ ἂν δίκαιον λόγον ἀντείποιμι, ὅτι

"οὐ καλῶς λέγεις, ὦ ἄνθρωπε, εἰ οἴει δεῖν κίνδυνον ὑπολογίζεσθαι τοῦ ζῆν ἢ τεθνάναι ἄνδρα ὅτου τι καὶ σμικρὸν ὄφελός ἐστιν, ἀλλ' οὐκ ἐκεῖνο μόνον σκοπεῖν ὅταν πράττῃ, πότερον δίκαια ἢ ἄδικα πράττει, καὶ ἀνδρὸς [28c] ἀγαθοῦ ἔργα ἢ κακοῦ. φαῦλοι γὰρ ἂν τῷ γε σῷ λόγῳ εἶεν τῶν ἡμιθέων ὅσοι ἐν Τροίᾳ τετελευτήκασιν οἵ τε ἄλλοι καὶ ὁ τῆς Θέτιδος ὑός, ὃς τοσοῦτον τοῦ κινδύνου κατεφρόνησεν παρὰ τὸ αἰσχρόν τι ὑπομεῖναι ὥστε, ἐπειδὴ εἶπεν ἡ μήτηρ αὐτῷ προθυμουμένῳ Ἕκτορα ἀποκτεῖναι, θεὸς οὖσα, οὑτωσί πως, ὡς ἐγὼ οἶμαι·

'ὦ παῖ, εἰ τιμωρήσεις Πατρόκλῳ τῷ ἑταίρῳ τὸν φόνον καὶ Ἕκτορα ἀποκτενεῖς, αὐτὸς ἀποθανῇ—
αὐτίκα γάρ τοι (φησί) μεθ' Ἕκτορα πότμος ἑτοῖμος'

—ὁ δὲ τοῦτο ἀκούσας τοῦ μὲν θανάτου καὶ τοῦ κινδύνου ὠλιγώρησε, πολὺ [28d] δὲ μᾶλλον δείσας τὸ ζῆν κακὸς ὢν καὶ τοῖς φίλοις μὴ τιμωρεῖν,

To that, however, I'd offer a straightforward response:

> "You're mistaken, sir, if you believe a man of any value should weigh the risk of living or dying when deciding what to do. The only consideration ought to be whether actions are just or unjust, whether they are the deeds of a good [28c] man or a bad one. Indeed, by your logic, all the demigod heroes who died at Troy, including Achilles, the son of Thetis, would seem foolish. Achilles so despised danger—rather than endure the shame of leaving Patroclus unavenged—that when he was intent on killing Hector, his mother, a goddess, said to him something like this:
>
> > 'Son, if you slay Hector to avenge the murder of your friend, you yourself will die—
> > *soon, because after Hector's, thine own doom is impending.*'[15]
>
> "He heard her warning but dismissed danger and death, for what he feared [28d] far more was failing to avenge his loved ones, and a life of disgrace. So he responded:

'αὐτίκα (φησί) τεθναίην, δίκην ἐπιθεὶς τῷ ἀδικοῦντι,
ἵνα μὴ ἐνθάδε μένω καταγέλαστος παρὰ νηυσὶ κορωνίσιν ἄχθος ἀρούρης.'

"μὴ αὐτὸν οἴει φροντίσαι θανάτου καὶ κινδύνου;"

οὕτω γὰρ ἔχει, ὦ ἄνδρες Ἀθηναῖοι, τῇ ἀληθείᾳ· οὗ ἄν τις ἑαυτὸν τάξῃ ἡγησάμενος βέλτιστον εἶναι ἢ ὑπ' ἄρχοντος ταχθῇ, ἐνταῦθα δεῖ, ὡς ἐμοὶ δοκεῖ, μένοντα κινδυνεύειν, μηδὲν ὑπολογιζόμενον μήτε θάνατον μήτε ἄλλο μηδὲν πρὸ τοῦ αἰσχροῦ.

ἐγὼ οὖν δεινὰ ἂν εἴην εἰργασμένος, ὦ ἄνδρες Ἀθηναῖοι, [28e] εἰ ὅτε μέν με οἱ ἄρχοντες ἔταττον, οὓς ὑμεῖς εἵλεσθε ἄρχειν μου, καὶ ἐν Ποτειδαίᾳ καὶ ἐν Ἀμφιπόλει καὶ ἐπὶ Δηλίῳ, τότε μὲν οὗ ἐκεῖνοι ἔταττον ἔμενον ὥσπερ καὶ ἄλλος τις καὶ ἐκινδύνευον ἀποθανεῖν, τοῦ δὲ θεοῦ τάττοντος, ὡς ἐγὼ ᾠήθην τε καὶ ὑπέλαβον, φιλοσοφοῦντά με δεῖν ζῆν καὶ ἐξετάζοντα ἐμαυτὸν καὶ τοὺς ἄλλους, [29a] ἐνταῦθα δὲ φοβηθεὶς ἢ θάνατον ἢ ἄλλ' ὁτιοῦν πρᾶγμα λίποιμι τὴν τάξιν. δεινόν τἂν εἴη, καὶ ὡς ἀληθῶς τότ' ἄν με δικαίως εἰσάγοι τις εἰς δικαστήριον, ὅτι οὐ νομίζω

> 'Let *me die soon!—provided I justly punish the culprit, rather than staying on here as a laughingstock beside the curved ships, a burden upon the earth.*'[16]

> "You don't really believe he was worried about death and danger, do you?"

That's how it should be for anyone, men of Athens. When you've chosen the place in life you believe is best, or when your commanding officer has assigned it to you, in my view you should *stay* there and face the consequences, come what may, whether it's death or anything else, rather than retreat in shame.[17]

So it would be disgraceful of me, men of Athens, [28e] if I—who stood firm in battle in my assigned place at Potidaea, at Amphipolis, and at Delium when commanded to do so by the leaders you elected to command me, and faced death like everybody else—if I were to abandon my post now out of fear of death or anything else—a post, mind you, that was assigned by the god who commanded me (as I felt sure he did) [29a] to live a life of freethought and examination of myself and others.[18] *That* would be disgraceful, and you would rightly haul me into court to accuse me of not believing in gods, since

θεοὺς εἶναι ἀπειθῶν τῇ μαντείᾳ καὶ δεδιὼς θάνατον καὶ οἰόμενος σοφὸς εἶναι οὐκ ὤν. τὸ γάρ τοι θάνατον δεδιέναι, ὦ ἄνδρες, οὐδὲν ἄλλο ἐστὶν ἢ δοκεῖν σοφὸν εἶναι μὴ ὄντα· δοκεῖν γὰρ εἰδέναι ἐστὶν ἃ οὐκ οἶδεν. οἶδε μὲν γὰρ οὐδεὶς τὸν θάνατον οὐδ' εἰ τυγχάνει τῷ ἀνθρώπῳ πάντων μέγιστον ὂν τῶν ἀγαθῶν, δεδίασι δ' ὡς εὖ εἰδότες ὅτι μέγιστον τῶν κακῶν ἐστι. [29b] καὶ τοῦτο πῶς οὐκ ἀμαθία ἐστὶν αὕτη ἡ ἐπονείδιστος, ἡ τοῦ οἴεσθαι εἰδέναι ἃ οὐκ οἶδεν;

ἐγὼ δ', ὦ ἄνδρες, τούτῳ καὶ ἐνταῦθα ἴσως διαφέρω τῶν πολλῶν ἀνθρώπων, καὶ εἰ δή τῳ σοφώτερός του φαίην εἶναι, τούτῳ ἄν, ὅτι οὐκ εἰδὼς ἱκανῶς περὶ τῶν ἐν Ἅιδου οὕτω καὶ οἴομαι οὐκ εἰδέναι· τὸ δὲ ἀδικεῖν καὶ ἀπειθεῖν τῷ βελτίονι καὶ θεῷ καὶ ἀνθρώπῳ, ὅτι κακὸν καὶ αἰσχρόν ἐστιν οἶδα. πρὸ οὖν τῶν κακῶν ὧν οἶδα ὅτι κακά ἐστιν, ἃ μὴ οἶδα εἰ καὶ ἀγαθὰ ὄντα τυγχάνει οὐδέποτε φοβήσομαι οὐδὲ φεύξομαι·

[29c] ὥστε οὐδ' εἴ με νῦν ὑμεῖς ἀφίετε Ἀνύτῳ ἀπιστήσαντες, ὃς ἔφη ἢ τὴν ἀρχὴν οὐ δεῖν ἐμὲ δεῦρο εἰσελθεῖν ἤ, ἐπειδὴ εἰσῆλθον, οὐχ οἷόν τ' εἶναι τὸ μὴ ἀποκτεῖναί με, λέγων πρὸς ὑμᾶς ὡς εἰ διαφευξοίμην, ἤδη ἂν ὑμῶν οἱ ὑεῖς ἐπιτηδεύοντες ἃ Σωκράτης διδάσκει πάντες παντάπασι διαφθαρήσονται—εἴ μοι πρὸς ταῦτα εἴποιτε·

I'd be disobeying the oracle and fearing death and imagining that I'm wise when I'm not. The truth is, gentlemen, fearing death is nothing more than believing you are wise when you aren't, since it means believing you know what you don't know. You see, nobody knows whether death might not be our greatest blessing, but people fear it as if they knew for certain that it's the greatest evil.[19] [29b] And isn't it a pathetic kind of ignorance to believe you know what you don't?

And here too perhaps I do differ from most people, gentlemen, and if I ever did claim to be wiser than others, it would be in this: that I don't know much about the world below, but I also don't think I do. I do know, however, that acting unjustly and disobeying a superior—whether god or man—is shameful and wrong. So I will never fear or avoid what for all I know might be good, just to escape the evils that I know are truly bad.

[29c] Accordingly, even if you let me go today and refuse to do the bidding of Anytus—who says I never should have showed up here in the first place[20] or else, since I have, that there is no choice but to have me put to death—because (as he put it to you), if I slip through your hands, your sons will soon all end up completely brainwashed and ruined by fol-

> “ὦ Σώκρατες, νῦν μὲν Ἀνύτῳ οὐ πεισόμεθα ἀλλ’ ἀφίεμέν σε, ἐπὶ τούτῳ μέντοι, ἐφ’ ᾧτε μηκέτι ἐν ταύτῃ τῇ ζητήσει διατρίβειν μηδὲ φιλοσοφεῖν· ἐὰν δὲ ἁλῷς ἔτι τοῦτο πράττων, [29d] ἀποθανῇ”

—εἰ οὖν με, ὅπερ εἶπον, ἐπὶ τούτοις ἀφίοιτε, εἴποιμ’ ἂν ὑμῖν ὅτι

> “ἐγὼ ὑμᾶς, ὦ ἄνδρες Ἀθηναῖοι, ἀσπάζομαι μὲν καὶ φιλῶ, πείσομαι δὲ μᾶλλον τῷ θεῷ ἢ ὑμῖν, καὶ ἕωσπερ ἂν ἐμπνέω καὶ οἷός τε ὦ, οὐ μὴ παύσωμαι φιλοσοφῶν καὶ ὑμῖν παρακελευόμενός τε καὶ ἐνδεικνύμενος ὅτῳ ἂν ἀεὶ ἐντυγχάνω ὑμῶν, λέγων οἷάπερ εἴωθα, ὅτι
>
> > ‘ὦ ἄριστε ἀνδρῶν, Ἀθηναῖος ὤν, πόλεως τῆς μεγίστης καὶ εὐδοκιμωτάτης εἰς σοφίαν καὶ ἰσχύν, χρημάτων μὲν οὐκ αἰσχύνῃ ἐπιμελούμενος ὅπως σοι ἔσται ὡς πλεῖστα, [29e] καὶ δόξης καὶ τιμῆς, φρονήσεως δὲ καὶ ἀληθείας καὶ τῆς ψυχῆς ὅπως ὡς βελτίστη ἔσται οὐκ ἐπιμελῇ οὐδὲ φροντίζεις;’

lowing Socrates's teachings—in the face of all that, if you were to say to me,

> "Socrates, we will not do the bidding of Anytus here today. We'll release you, but only on condition that you spend no more time on this investigation and you stop thinking for yourself; and if you're caught doing it again, [29d] you will be put to death."

If you let me off on these terms, as I said, I'd tell you this:

> "I love and respect you, men of Athens, but I will obey the god rather than you. And as long as I have breath and strength, I will not stop thinking for myself, nor will I ever cease to exhort and question any one of you I meet. I'll continue to say, as I always have,
>
> > 'Best of men, you are a citizen of Athens, a city greater and more renowned for wisdom and power than any other. Aren't you ashamed to care so much about getting rich [29e] and your reputation and honor, but for wisdom and truth and your soul—that you make it the best it

καὶ ἐάν τις ὑμῶν ἀμφισβητήσῃ καὶ φῇ ἐπιμελεῖσθαι, οὐκ εὐθὺς ἀφήσω αὐτὸν οὐδ' ἄπειμι, ἀλλ' ἐρήσομαι αὐτὸν καὶ ἐξετάσω καὶ ἐλέγξω, καὶ ἐάν μοι μὴ δοκῇ κεκτῆσθαι ἀρετήν, [30a] φάναι δέ, ὀνειδιῶ ὅτι τὰ πλείστου ἄξια περὶ ἐλαχίστου ποιεῖται, τὰ δὲ φαυλότερα περὶ πλείονος. ταῦτα καὶ νεωτέρῳ καὶ πρεσβυτέρῳ ὅτῳ ἂν ἐντυγχάνω ποιήσω, καὶ ξένῳ καὶ ἀστῷ, μᾶλλον δὲ τοῖς ἀστοῖς, ὅσῳ μου ἐγγυτέρω ἐστὲ γένει. ταῦτα γὰρ κελεύει ὁ θεός, εὖ ἴστε, καὶ ἐγὼ οἴομαι οὐδέν πω ὑμῖν μεῖζον ἀγαθὸν γενέσθαι ἐν τῇ πόλει ἢ τὴν ἐμὴν τῷ θεῷ ὑπηρεσίαν. οὐδὲν γὰρ ἄλλο πράττων ἐγὼ περιέρχομαι ἢ πείθων ὑμῶν καὶ νεωτέρους καὶ πρεσβυτέρους μήτε σωμάτων ἐπιμελεῖσθαι [30b] μήτε χρημάτων πρότερον μηδὲ οὕτω σφόδρα ὡς τῆς ψυχῆς ὅπως ὡς ἀρίστη ἔσται, λέγων ὅτι

> 'οὐκ ἐκ χρημάτων ἀρετὴ γίγνεται, ἀλλ' ἐξ ἀρετῆς χρήματα καὶ τὰ ἄλλα ἀγαθὰ τοῖς ἀνθρώποις ἅπαντα καὶ ἰδίᾳ καὶ δημοσίᾳ.'

> can be—you don't care or think about that at all?'

"And if any of you dispute this and claim you do care, I won't just let you off or leave without interrogating and examining and refuting you. And if I find the integrity you claim for yourself [30a] isn't there, I will rebuke you for valuing the most important thing in the world the least, and paltrier matters more. This I will do for any I meet, whether young or old, whether citizen or foreigner—though especially you, my fellow citizens, because you're more closely related to me. This is the god's command—you must understand this—and I firmly believe that no greater benefit has ever come to you in this city than my devoted service to the god. See, I do nothing else but go around trying to persuade you, young and old alike, not to care more about your bodies [30b] or money, or so passionately, as about your soul, so it will be the finest that it can. I tell you:

> 'Integrity comes not from money, but from integrity comes money and all else that is good for human beings in their private and public lives.'

εἰ μὲν οὖν ταῦτα λέγων διαφθείρω τοὺς νέους, ταῦτ' ἂν εἴη βλαβερά· εἰ δέ τίς μέ φησιν ἄλλα λέγειν ἢ ταῦτα, οὐδὲν λέγει. πρὸς ταῦτα,"

φαίην ἄν,

"ὦ ἄνδρες Ἀθηναῖοι, ἢ πείθεσθε Ἀνύτῳ ἢ μή, καὶ ἢ ἀφίετέ με ἢ μὴ ἀφίετε, [30c] ὡς ἐμοῦ οὐκ ἂν ποιήσαντος ἄλλα, οὐδ' εἰ μέλλω πολλάκις τεθνάναι."

μὴ θορυβεῖτε, ὦ ἄνδρες Ἀθηναῖοι, ἀλλ' ἐμμείνατέ μοι οἷς ἐδεήθην ὑμῶν, μὴ θορυβεῖν ἐφ' οἷς ἂν λέγω ἀλλ' ἀκούειν· καὶ γάρ, ὡς ἐγὼ οἶμαι, ὀνήσεσθε ἀκούοντες. μέλλω γὰρ οὖν ἄττα ὑμῖν ἐρεῖν καὶ ἄλλα ἐφ' οἷς ἴσως βοήσεσθε· ἀλλὰ μηδαμῶς ποιεῖτε τοῦτο.

εὖ γὰρ ἴστε, ἐάν με ἀποκτείνητε τοιοῦτον ὄντα οἷον ἐγὼ λέγω, οὐκ ἐμὲ μείζω βλάψετε ἢ ὑμᾶς αὐτούς·

ἐμὲ μὲν γὰρ οὐδὲν ἂν βλάψειεν οὔτε Μέλητος οὔτε Ἄνυτος· οὐδὲ γὰρ ἂν δύναιτο· [30d] οὐ γὰρ

> "If I'm brainwashing the youth by saying this, then it must be the case that these words are harmful. But if anyone claims I say something *different*, that's nonsense. Considering this,"

I'd say,

> "men of Athens, you may choose to do Anytus's bidding or not, to let me go or not. [30c] But do know that I will not change my ways, even if it means being put to death many times over."[21]

Sounds of indignation begin to rise.

Please, men of Athens, no shouting! I ask you once more, as I did earlier: listen calmly to what I have to say and don't start shouting. I really do think it's in your best interest to hear me out, and I'm about to say some other things that might upset some of you. I beg you not to shout me down.

You see, you must understand that if you put me to death, as I am—a person like the one I claim to be—you won't be harming me more than you'll harm yourselves.[22]

Neither Meletus nor Anytus can truly harm me. That's impossible, [30d] because I do not believe the

οἴομαι θεμιτὸν εἶναι ἀμείνονι ἀνδρὶ ὑπὸ χείρονος βλάπτεσθαι. ἀποκτείνειε μεντἂν ἴσως ἢ ἐξελάσειεν ἢ ἀτιμώσειεν· ἀλλὰ ταῦτα οὗτος μὲν ἴσως οἴεται καὶ ἄλλος τίς που μεγάλα κακά, ἐγὼ δ' οὐκ οἴομαι, ἀλλὰ πολὺ μᾶλλον ποιεῖν ἃ οὑτοσὶ νῦν ποιεῖ, ἄνδρα ἀδίκως ἐπιχειρεῖν ἀποκτεινύναι.

νῦν οὖν, ὦ ἄνδρες Ἀθηναῖοι, πολλοῦ δέω ἐγὼ ὑπὲρ ἐμαυτοῦ ἀπολογεῖσθαι, ὥς τις ἂν οἴοιτο, ἀλλὰ ὑπὲρ ὑμῶν, μή τι ἐξαμάρτητε περὶ τὴν τοῦ θεοῦ δόσιν ὑμῖν ἐμοῦ καταψηφισάμενοι. [30e] ἐὰν γάρ με ἀποκτείνητε, οὐ ῥᾳδίως ἄλλον τοιοῦτον εὑρήσετε, ἀτεχνῶς, εἰ καὶ γελοιότερον εἰπεῖν, προσκείμενον τῇ πόλει ὑπὸ τοῦ θεοῦ ὥσπερ ἵππῳ μεγάλῳ μὲν καὶ γενναίῳ, ὑπὸ μεγέθους δὲ νωθεστέρῳ καὶ δεομένῳ ἐγείρεσθαι ὑπὸ μύωπός τινος· οἷον δή μοι δοκεῖ ὁ θεὸς ἐμὲ τῇ πόλει προστεθηκέναι—τοιοῦτόν τινα ὃς ὑμᾶς ἐγείρων καὶ πείθων καὶ ὀνειδίζων [31a] ἕνα ἕκαστον οὐδὲν παύομαι τὴν ἡμέραν ὅλην πανταχοῦ προσκαθίζων. τοιοῦτος οὖν ἄλλος οὐ ῥᾳδίως ὑμῖν γενήσεται, ὦ ἄνδρες, ἀλλ' ἐὰν ἐμοὶ πείθησθε, φείσεσθέ μου· ὑμεῖς δ' ἴσως τάχ' ἂν ἀχθόμενοι, ὥσπερ οἱ νυστάζοντες ἐγειρόμενοι, κρούσαντες ἄν με, πειθόμενοι Ἀνύτῳ, ῥᾳδίως ἂν ἀποκτείναιτε, εἶτα τὸν λοιπὸν βίον καθεύδοντες διατελοῖτε ἄν, εἰ μή τινα ἄλλον ὁ θεὸς ὑμῖν ἐπιπέμψειεν κηδόμενος ὑμῶν.

gods allow a worse man to harm a better one. Oh, he can obviously kill me, banish me, or strip me of my rights, and he and others may believe these are grave harms. But I don't.[23] What's truly harmful is what he's doing now: attempting to get an innocent man put to death.

So, men of Athens, I'm not here defending myself, as one might suppose. I'm defending *you*—to prevent you from making a terrible mistake about the god's gift to you, which is what you'll do if you find me guilty. [30e] If you kill me, see, you won't easily find another like me. That's because—and this might sound a little funny—the god has literally attached me to this city of ours, which is like a magnificent, muscular horse that's gotten muscle bound and lethargic and needs some gadfly to jolt it awake. I believe the god has attached me to this city as something like that. I jolt and pester and reproach [31a] each and every one of you, and I don't stop—landing on you all day long, wherever I can. You won't easily get another like me, gentlemen, so if you do as I ask, you'll spare my life. Now, you may well feel annoyed, like someone being shaken awake from a nap, and want to swat at me. If you follow Anytus's advice, you'd have no trouble killing me. If you do, you'll return to your sleepy ways for the

ὅτι δ᾽ ἐγὼ τυγχάνω ὢν τοιοῦτος οἷος ὑπὸ τοῦ θεοῦ τῇ πόλει δεδόσθαι, ἐνθένδε ἂν κατανοήσαιτε· [31b] οὐ γὰρ ἀνθρωπίνῳ ἔοικε τὸ ἐμὲ τῶν μὲν ἐμαυτοῦ πάντων ἠμεληκέναι καὶ ἀνέχεσθαι τῶν οἰκείων ἀμελουμένων τοσαῦτα ἤδη ἔτη, τὸ δὲ ὑμέτερον πράττειν ἀεί, ἰδίᾳ ἑκάστῳ προσιόντα ὥσπερ πατέρα ἢ ἀδελφὸν πρεσβύτερον πείθοντα ἐπιμελεῖσθαι ἀρετῆς. καὶ εἰ μέν τι ἀπὸ τούτων ἀπέλαυον καὶ μισθὸν λαμβάνων ταῦτα παρεκελευόμην, εἶχον ἄν τινα λόγον· νῦν δὲ ὁρᾶτε δὴ καὶ αὐτοὶ ὅτι οἱ κατήγοροι τἆλλα πάντα ἀναισχύντως οὕτω κατηγοροῦντες, τοῦτό γε οὐχ οἷοί τε ἐγένοντο ἀπαναισχυντῆσαι παρασχόμενοι μάρτυρα, [31c] ὡς ἐγώ ποτέ τινα ἢ ἐπραξάμην μισθὸν ἢ ᾔτησα. ἱκανὸν γάρ, οἶμαι, ἐγὼ παρέχομαι τὸν μάρτυρα ὡς ἀληθῆ λέγω, τὴν πενίαν.

ἴσως ἂν οὖν δόξειεν ἄτοπον εἶναι, ὅτι δὴ ἐγὼ ἰδίᾳ μὲν ταῦτα συμβουλεύω περιιὼν καὶ πολυπραγμονῶ, δημοσίᾳ δὲ οὐ τολμῶ ἀναβαίνων εἰς τὸ πλῆθος τὸ ὑμέτερον συμβουλεύειν τῇ πόλει. τούτου δὲ αἴτιόν ἐστιν ὃ ὑμεῖς ἐμοῦ πολλάκις ἀκηκόατε πολλαχοῦ λέγοντος, ὅτι μοι θεῖόν τι καὶ δαιμόνιον γίγνεται, [31d] ὃ δὴ καὶ ἐν τῇ γραφῇ ἐπικωμῳδῶν Μέλητος

rest of your lives—unless the god, in his love for you, decides to send you someone else.[24]

You can understand that I'm the kind of person for the god to have bestowed upon the city as a gift from this [31b], that it just doesn't seem *human* for me to have neglected my whole life and endured the neglect of my family all these years—and devoted myself entirely to *your* interests instead. I am perpetually going to each of you in private, like a father or older brother, and urging you to care about integrity. If I were getting anything from all this—if I were charging tuition for encouraging people in this way—then I'd have some justification for it. But as you yourselves can see, my accusers have made all sorts of shameless claims, but they couldn't stoop so low as to bring forward a single witness to testify that [31c] I ever asked for or accepted payment. As a matter of fact, I've brought you the best witness I can to prove I'm telling the truth: my poverty.

Now, some might think it strange that I go around giving advice to people privately and involving myself in their lives, but I don't dare step out into your midst and advise the city as a whole. There's a reason for that, and you have heard me explain it many times before: I have something divine and angelic that comes to me—[31d] it's what Meletus mocked in that complaint of his. I started

ἐγράψατο. ἐμοὶ δὲ τοῦτ' ἔστιν ἐκ παιδὸς ἀρξάμενον, φωνή τις γιγνομένη, ἣ ὅταν γένηται, ἀεὶ ἀποτρέπει με τοῦτο ὃ ἂν μέλλω πράττειν, προτρέπει δὲ οὔποτε. τοῦτ' ἔστιν ὅ μοι ἐναντιοῦται τὰ πολιτικὰ πράττειν, καὶ παγκάλως γέ μοι δοκεῖ ἐναντιοῦσθαι·

εὖ γὰρ ἴστε, ὦ ἄνδρες Ἀθηναῖοι, εἰ ἐγὼ πάλαι ἐπεχείρησα πράττειν τὰ πολιτικὰ πράγματα, πάλαι ἂν ἀπολώλη καὶ οὔτ' ἂν ὑμᾶς ὠφελήκη οὐδὲν [31e] οὔτ' ἂν ἐμαυτόν. καί μοι μὴ ἄχθεσθε λέγοντι τἀληθῆ· οὐ γὰρ ἔστιν ὅστις ἀνθρώπων σωθήσεται οὔτε ὑμῖν οὔτε ἄλλῳ πλήθει οὐδενὶ γνησίως ἐναντιούμενος καὶ διακωλύων πολλὰ ἄδικα καὶ παράνομα ἐν τῇ πόλει γίγνεσθαι, [32a] ἀλλ' ἀναγκαῖόν ἐστι τὸν τῷ ὄντι μαχούμενον ὑπὲρ τοῦ δικαίου, καὶ εἰ μέλλει ὀλίγον χρόνον σωθήσεσθαι, ἰδιωτεύειν ἀλλὰ μὴ δημοσιεύειν.

μεγάλα δ' ἔγωγε ὑμῖν τεκμήρια παρέξομαι τούτων, οὐ λόγους, ἀλλ' ὃ ὑμεῖς τιμᾶτε, ἔργα. ἀκούσατε δή μοι τὰ συμβεβηκότα, ἵνα εἰδῆτε ὅτι οὐδ' ἂν ἑνὶ ὑπεικάθοιμι παρὰ τὸ δίκαιον δείσας θάνατον, μὴ ὑπείκων δὲ ἅμα κἂν ἀπολοίμην. ἐρῶ δὲ ὑμῖν φορτικὰ μὲν καὶ δικανικά, ἀληθῆ δέ.

ἐγὼ γάρ, ὦ ἄνδρες Ἀθηναῖοι, ἄλλην [32b] μὲν ἀρχὴν οὐδεμίανπώποτε ἦρξα ἐν τῇ πόλει, ἐβούλευσα δέ· καὶ ἔτυχεν ἡμῶν ἡ φυλὴ Ἀντιοχὶς πρυτανεύουσα ὅτε ὑμεῖς

getting it in childhood; it comes as a kind of voice. When it does, it always stops me from doing something I'm about to do, but it never encourages me to take action. This is what prevents me from getting involved in politics, and I believe it's entirely right to do so.

You see, men of Athens, you must understand that if I'd tried to get involved in political activity, I'd have wound up dead long ago and been of no use to you [31e] or myself. So do not take offense when I state the simple truth: that no man will survive this or any other group if he opposes you in good faith and seeks to curb the many injustices and abuses within. [32a] A man who truly fights for justice must lead a private life, not a public one, if he is to survive for even a short time.

I'll give you strong evidence of this—and not just words, but actions, which I know you value. Listen to what happened to me, so you can see that fear of death would never make me comply with an unjust order from anyone, not even if refusing it meant losing my life. What I'm about to tell you may sound like a typical emotional appeal, but it's the truth.

Men of Athens, I've never [32b] held any public office in the city, but I have served as a member of the Council of 500. It so happened that our tribe, Antiochis, was presiding when you resolved to put

τοὺς δέκα στρατηγοὺς τοὺς οὐκ ἀνελομένους τοὺς ἐκ τῆς ναυμαχίας ἐβουλεύσασθε ἁθρόους κρίνειν, παρανόμως, ὡς ἐν τῷ ὑστέρῳ χρόνῳ πᾶσιν ὑμῖν ἔδοξεν. τότ' ἐγὼ μόνος τῶν πρυτάνεων ἠναντιώθην ὑμῖν μηδὲν ποιεῖν παρὰ τοὺς νόμους καὶ ἐναντία ἐψηφισάμην· καὶ ἑτοίμων ὄντων ἐνδεικνύναι με καὶ ἀπάγειν τῶν ῥητόρων, καὶ ὑμῶν κελευόντων καὶ βοώντων, μετὰ τοῦ νόμου καὶ τοῦ δικαίου [32c] ᾤμην μᾶλλόν με δεῖν διακινδυνεύειν ἢ μεθ' ὑμῶν γενέσθαι μὴ δίκαια βουλευομένων, φοβηθέντα δεσμὸν ἢ θάνατον.

καὶ ταῦτα μὲν ἦν ἔτι δημοκρατουμένης τῆς πόλεως· ἐπειδὴ δὲ ὀλιγαρχία ἐγένετο, οἱ τριάκοντα αὖ μεταπεμψάμενοί με πέμπτον αὐτὸν εἰς τὴν θόλον προσέταξαν ἀγαγεῖν ἐκ Σαλαμῖνος Λέοντα τὸν Σαλαμίνιον ἵνα ἀποθάνοι· οἷα δὴ καὶ ἄλλοις ἐκεῖνοι πολλοῖς πολλὰ προσέταττον, βουλόμενοι ὡς πλείστους ἀναπλῆσαι αἰτιῶν. τότε μέντοι ἐγὼ οὐ [32d] λόγῳ ἀλλ' ἔργῳ αὖ ἐνεδειξάμην ὅτι ἐμοὶ θανάτου μὲν μέλει, εἰ μὴ ἀγροικότερον ἦν εἰπεῖν, οὐδ' ὁτιοῦν, τοῦ δὲ μηδὲν ἄδικον μηδ' ἀνόσιον ἐργάζεσθαι, τούτου δὲ τὸ πᾶν μέλει. ἐμὲ γὰρ ἐκείνη ἡ ἀρχὴ οὐκ ἐξέπληξεν, οὕτως ἰσχυρὰ οὖσα, ὥστε ἄδικόν τι ἐργάσασθαι, ἀλλ' ἐπειδὴ ἐκ τῆς θόλου ἐξήλθομεν, οἱ μὲν τέτταρες ᾤχοντο εἰς Σαλαμῖνα καὶ ἤγαγον Λέοντα, ἐγὼ δὲ ᾠχόμην ἀπιὼν

those ten generals on trial who'd failed to rescue their sailors after the naval battle. You wanted to try them en masse, which was illegal—a fact you all later acknowledged. At the time, I was the only member of the presiding Council who stood up against you and refused to go against the law. I voted against it, even though the political leaders were ready to denounce and drag me away, and despite your piling pressure on me to go along. I believed it was better to side with justice and the law [32c] and take my chances than to join you in injustice out of fear of prison or death.[25]

That was back during the democracy. Later, when the oligarchy of The Thirty came to power, they summoned me and four others to the Rotunda and ordered us to bring Leon of Salamis in from Salamis for execution.[26] They issued many orders like that, wanting to implicate as many people as possible in their crimes. On that occasion I [32d] again showed through my actions—not just my words—that I couldn't care less about death (if that's not putting it too bluntly). The only thing I care about is never doing anything unjust or immoral in the eyes of the gods. And so despite the power of that regime, it wasn't enough to terrify *me* into committing an injustice. When we left the Rotunda, the other four went off to Salamis and arrested Leon, but I left and

οἴκαδε. καὶ ἴσως ἂν διὰ ταῦτα ἀπέθανον, εἰ μὴ ἡ ἀρχὴ διὰ ταχέων κατελύθη. [32e] καὶ τούτων ὑμῖν ἔσονται πολλοὶ μάρτυρες.

ἆρ' οὖν ἄν με οἴεσθε τοσάδε ἔτη διαγενέσθαι εἰ ἔπραττον τὰ δημόσια, καὶ πράττων ἀξίως ἀνδρὸς ἀγαθοῦ ἐβοήθουν τοῖς δικαίοις καί, ὥσπερ χρή, τοῦτο περὶ πλείστου ἐποιούμην; πολλοῦ γε δεῖ, ὦ ἄνδρες Ἀθηναῖοι· [33a] οὐδὲ γὰρ ἂν ἄλλος ἀνθρώπων οὐδείς. ἀλλ' ἐγὼ διὰ παντὸς τοῦ βίου δημοσίᾳ τε εἴ πού τι ἔπραξα τοιοῦτος φανοῦμαι, καὶ ἰδίᾳ ὁ αὐτὸς οὗτος, οὐδενὶ πώποτε συγχωρήσας οὐδὲν παρὰ τὸ δίκαιον οὔτε ἄλλῳ οὔτε τούτων οὐδενὶ οὓς δὴ διαβάλλοντες ἐμέ φασιν ἐμοὺς μαθητὰς εἶναι. ἐγὼ δὲ διδάσκαλος μὲν οὐδενὸς πώποτ' ἐγενόμην· εἰ δέ τίς μου λέγοντος καὶ τὰ ἐμαυτοῦ πράττοντος ἐπιθυμοῖ ἀκούειν, εἴτε νεώτερος εἴτε πρεσβύτερος, οὐδενὶ πώποτε ἐφθόνησα, [33b] οὐδὲ χρήματα μὲν λαμβάνων διαλέγομαι μὴ λαμβάνων δὲ οὔ, ἀλλ' ὁμοίως καὶ πλουσίῳ καὶ πένητι παρέχω ἐμαυτὸν ἐρωτᾶν, καὶ ἐάν τις βούληται ἀποκρινόμενος ἀκούειν ὧν ἂν λέγω. καὶ τούτων ἐγὼ εἴτε τις χρηστὸς γίγνεται εἴτε μή, οὐκ ἂν δικαίως τὴν αἰτίαν ὑπέχοιμι, ὧν μήτε ὑπεσχόμην

went home. And I might well have been executed for doing that, if the regime hadn't fallen so soon after. [32e] There are many witnesses who can confirm what I've just told you.

Witnesses step forward to verify Socrates's statement.

Do you really think I could have survived all these years if I'd been involved in public affairs, standing up for justice as a good man should and making it my top priority? Not a chance, men of Athens [33a]—no one could. All my life, both in public when I've been involved in anything, it should be obvious that this is how I am, and in private, I have always acted the same way: I have never compromised what's right for anyone, not for any person or group, including those whom my demonizers claim are students of mine. I have never been anyone's teacher. If anyone, young or old, wants to listen while I'm talking and doing my thing, I have never turned them away. [33b] I don't charge money to have a conversation, or refuse a conversation because I don't. No, I allow rich and poor alike to question me, and, if anyone chooses to respond, to then hear what I say next. Whether someone improves because of this or not, I can't

μηδενὶ μηδὲν πώποτε μάθημα μήτε ἐδίδαξα· εἰ δέ τίς φησι παρ' ἐμοῦ πώποτέ τι μαθεῖν ἢ ἀκοῦσαι ἰδίᾳ ὅτι μὴ καὶ οἱ ἄλλοι πάντες, εὖ ἴστε ὅτι οὐκ ἀληθῆ λέγει.

ἀλλὰ διὰ τί δή ποτε μετ' ἐμοῦ χαίρουσί τινες πολὺν χρόνον διατρίβοντες; [33c] ἀκηκόατε, ὦ ἄνδρες Ἀθηναῖοι· πᾶσαν ὑμῖν τὴν ἀλήθειαν ἐγὼ εἶπον· ὅτι ἀκούοντες χαίρουσιν ἐξεταζομένοις τοῖς οἰομένοις μὲν εἶναι σοφοῖς, οὖσι δ' οὔ. ἔστι γὰρ οὐκ ἀηδές. ἐμοὶ δὲ τοῦτο, ὡς ἐγώ φημι, προστέτακται ὑπὸ τοῦ θεοῦ πράττειν καὶ ἐκ μαντείων καὶ ἐξ ἐνυπνίων καὶ παντὶ τρόπῳ ᾧπέρ τίς ποτε καὶ ἄλλη θεία μοῖρα ἀνθρώπῳ καὶ ὁτιοῦν προσέταξε πράττειν.

ταῦτα, ὦ ἄνδρες Ἀθηναῖοι, καὶ ἀληθῆ ἐστιν καὶ εὐέλεγκτα. [33d] εἰ γὰρ δὴ ἔγωγε τῶν νέων τοὺς μὲν διαφθείρω τοὺς δὲ διέφθαρκα, χρῆν δήπου, εἴτε τινὲς αὐτῶν πρεσβύτεροι γενόμενοι ἔγνωσαν ὅτι νέοις οὖσιν αὐτοῖς ἐγὼ κακὸν πώποτέ τι συνεβούλευσα, νυνὶ αὐτοὺς ἀναβαίνοντας ἐμοῦ κατηγορεῖν καὶ τιμωρεῖσθαι· εἰ δὲ μὴ αὐτοὶ ἤθελον, τῶν οἰκείων τινὰς τῶν ἐκείνων, πατέρας καὶ ἀδελφοὺς καὶ ἄλλους τοὺς προσήκοντας, εἴπερ ὑπ' ἐμοῦ τι κακὸν ἐπεπόνθεσαν αὐτῶν οἱ οἰκεῖοι, νῦν μεμνῆσθαι καὶ τιμωρεῖσθαι.

πάντως δὲ πάρεισιν αὐτῶν πολλοὶ ἐνταυθοῖ οὓς ἐγὼ ὁρῶ, πρῶτον μὲν Κρίτων οὑτοσί, ἐμὸς ἡλικιώτης καὶ δημότης, [33e] Κριτοβούλου τοῦδε πατήρ, ἔπειτα

reasonably be held responsible for matters I never promised to teach or did teach anyone a lesson in. And if anyone claims they've ever learned or heard something privately from me that others didn't, do know that they aren't telling the truth.

Why, then, *do* some people like spending so much time with me? [33c] You've heard the answer, men of Athens—I've told you the whole truth: they enjoy hearing those who think they're wise—but aren't—being questioned. It really is quite entertaining. For me, though, as I've said, this is something the god has commanded me to do—in oracles, dreams, and every other way the gods' plan commands us mortals to do anything at all.

It's true, men of Athens, and it's easy to prove. [33d] You see, if I really do brainwash the youth, or if I brainwashed them in the past, then now that they're older, wouldn't some of them have realized I gave them bad advice in their youth and come forward now to expose me and demand justice? Or if they didn't want to, surely some of their relatives—fathers, brothers, or other family members—would remember it now and demand justice, if I'd actually victimized their loved ones.

Yet here we are, and many of them are here right now, and I see them here among you: Crito, who is my own age and a fellow tribesman [33e] and

Λυσανίας ὁ Σφήττιος, Αἰσχίνου τοῦδε πατήρ, ἔτι δ᾽ Ἀντιφῶν ὁ Κηφισιεὺς οὑτοσί, Ἐπιγένους πατήρ, ἄλλοι τοίνυν οὗτοι ὧν οἱ ἀδελφοὶ ἐν ταύτῃ τῇ διατριβῇ γεγόνασιν, Νικόστρατος Θεοζοτίδου, ἀδελφὸς Θεοδότου—καὶ ὁ μὲν Θεόδοτος τετελεύτηκεν, ὥστε οὐκ ἂν ἐκεῖνός γε αὐτοῦ καταδεηθείη—καὶ Παράλιος ὅδε, ὁ Δημοδόκου, οὗ ἦν Θεάγης ἀδελφός· [34a] ὅδε δὲ Ἀδείμαντος, ὁ Ἀρίστωνος, οὗ ἀδελφὸς οὑτοσὶ Πλάτων, καὶ Αἰαντόδωρος, οὗ Ἀπολλόδωρος ὅδε ἀδελφός.

καὶ ἄλλους πολλοὺς ἐγὼ ἔχω ὑμῖν εἰπεῖν, ὧν τινα ἐχρῆν μάλιστα μὲν ἐν τῷ ἑαυτοῦ λόγῳ παρασχέσθαι Μέλητον μάρτυρα· εἰ δὲ τότε ἐπελάθετο, νῦν παρασχέσθω—ἐγὼ παραχωρῶ—καὶ λεγέτω εἴ τι ἔχει τοιοῦτον.

ἀλλὰ τούτου πᾶν τοὐναντίον εὑρήσετε, ὦ ἄνδρες, πάντας ἐμοὶ βοηθεῖν ἑτοίμους τῷ διαφθείροντι, τῷ κακὰ ἐργαζομένῳ τοὺς οἰκείους αὐτῶν, ὥς φασι Μέλητος καὶ Ἄνυτος. [34b] αὐτοὶ μὲν γὰρ οἱ διεφθαρμένοι τάχ᾽ ἂν λόγον ἔχοιεν βοηθοῦντες· οἱ δὲ ἀδιάφθαρτοι, πρεσβύτεροι ἤδη ἄνδρες, οἱ τούτων

the father of Critobulus here; Lysanias of Sphettus, the father of Aeschines here; and Antiphon of Cephisia, the father of Epigenes. Then there are others here whose brothers were involved in our pastime. There's Nicostratus, the son of Theozotides, the brother of Theodotus (and Theodotus has passed away, by the way, so he at least isn't stopping Nicostratus), and Paralius, the son of Demodocus, whose brother is Theages. [34a] Here, too, is Adeimantus, the son of Ariston, whose brother is Plato here, and Aiantodorus, whose brother is Apollodorus here.

There are many others I could mention, and if Meletus were telling the truth he should have called any one of them as a witness in his opening statement. If he forgot to then, let's have him do so now—I'll step aside. Let him say if he has any such witness.

Meletus says nothing.

No, you'll find the complete opposite is true, gentlemen. All of them are ready to support me, the "brainwasher," the "victimizer" of their relatives, as Meletus and Anytus put it. [34b] Of course, those who have been brainwashed might very well speak in my favor; but what about the non-brainwashed—their

προσήκοντες, τίνα ἄλλον ἔχουσι λόγον βοηθοῦντες ἐμοὶ ἀλλ' ἢ τὸν ὀρθόν τε καὶ δίκαιον, ὅτι συνίσασι Μελήτῳ μὲν ψευδομένῳ, ἐμοὶ δὲ ἀληθεύοντι;

εἶεν δή, ὦ ἄνδρες· ἃ μὲν ἐγὼ ἔχοιμ' ἂν ἀπολογεῖσθαι, σχεδόν ἐστι ταῦτα καὶ ἄλλα ἴσως τοιαῦτα. [34c] τάχα δ' ἄν τις ὑμῶν ἀγανακτήσειεν ἀναμνησθεὶς ἑαυτοῦ, εἰ ὁ μὲν καὶ ἐλάττω τουτουῒ τοῦ ἀγῶνος ἀγῶνα ἀγωνιζόμενος ἐδεήθη τε καὶ ἱκέτευσε τοὺς δικαστὰς μετὰ πολλῶν δακρύων, παιδία τε αὑτοῦ ἀναβιβασάμενος ἵνα ὅτι μάλιστα ἐλεηθείη, καὶ ἄλλους τῶν οἰκείων καὶ φίλων πολλούς, ἐγὼ δὲ οὐδὲν ἄρα τούτων ποιήσω, καὶ ταῦτα κινδυνεύων, ὡς ἂν δόξαιμι, τὸν ἔσχατον κίνδυνον. τάχ' ἂν οὖν τις ταῦτα ἐννοήσας αὐθαδέστερον ἂν πρός με σχοίη καὶ ὀργισθεὶς αὐτοῖς [34d] τούτοις θεῖτο ἂν μετ' ὀργῆς τὴν ψῆφον. εἰ δή τις ὑμῶν οὕτως ἔχει—οὐκ ἀξιῶ μὲν γὰρ ἔγωγε, εἰ δ' οὖν—ἐπιεικῆ ἄν μοι δοκῶ πρὸς τοῦτον λέγειν λέγων ὅτι

> "ἐμοί, ὦ ἄριστε, εἰσὶν μέν πού τινες καὶ οἰκεῖοι· καὶ γὰρ τοῦτο αὐτὸ τὸ τοῦ Ὁμήρου, οὐδ' ἐγὼ 'ἀπὸ δρυὸς οὐδ' ἀπὸ πέτρης' πέφυκα ἀλλ' ἐξ ἀνθρώπων, ὥστε καὶ οἰκεῖοί μοί εἰσι καὶ ὑεῖς γε, ὦ ἄνδρες Ἀθηναῖοι, τρεῖς, εἷς μὲν μειράκιον ἤδη, δύο δὲ παιδία· ἀλλ' ὅμως οὐδένα αὐτῶν δεῦρο ἀναβιβασάμενος δεήσομαι ὑμῶν ἀποψηφίσασθαι."

relatives, older men now? What reason could *they* have to support me other than the right and just one: that they know full well Meletus is lying, and that I am telling the truth?

Well, gentlemen, this—and perhaps a few similar thoughts—is about all I had to say in my defense. [34c] It's possible one or two of you may feel resentful as you think back to your own conduct—when you were on trial in less momentous cases, and you sobbed and begged and pleaded with the jury and paraded your children and friends and relatives up here on the stand in order to garner all the sympathy you could. I'm not going to do any of that, even though I'm facing what could very well be the ultimate danger. So it's possible some of you will feel frustrated and get angry, and [34d] vote against me in anger. If that's how any man among you feels—I'm not saying anyone does, of course, but just in case—then I think it's fair to explain myself. I'd tell him,

> "Yes, I have a family, good sir. As Homer puts it, I wasn't born 'from an oak or a rock,'[27] but from humans. So I do have a family, men of Athens, including three sons—one a young man and the other two still children. Yet even so, I won't parade them up here while I plead for your acquittal."

τί δὴ οὖν οὐδὲν τούτων ποιήσω; οὐκ αὐθαδιζόμενος, ὦ ἄνδρες Ἀθηναῖοι, [34e] οὐδ' ὑμᾶς ἀτιμάζων· ἀλλ' εἰ μὲν θαρραλέως ἐγὼ ἔχω πρὸς θάνατον ἢ μή, ἄλλος λόγος, πρὸς δ' οὖν δόξαν καὶ ἐμοὶ καὶ ὑμῖν καὶ ὅλῃ τῇ πόλει οὔ μοι δοκεῖ καλὸν εἶναι ἐμὲ τούτων οὐδὲν ποιεῖν καὶ τηλικόνδε ὄντα καὶ τοῦτο τοὔνομα ἔχοντα—εἴτ' οὖν ἀληθὲς εἴτ' οὖν ψεῦδος, ἀλλ' οὖν δεδογμένον γέ ἐστί [35a] τῳ Σωκράτη διαφέρειν τινὶ τῶν πολλῶν ἀνθρώπων. εἰ οὖν ὑμῶν οἱ δοκοῦντες διαφέρειν εἴτε σοφίᾳ εἴτε ἀνδρείᾳ εἴτε ἄλλῃ ᾑτινιοῦν ἀρετῇ τοιοῦτοι ἔσονται, αἰσχρὸν ἂν εἴη· οἵουσπερ ἐγὼ πολλάκις ἑώρακά τινας ὅταν κρίνωνται, δοκοῦντας μέν τι εἶναι, θαυμάσια δὲ ἐργαζομένους, ὡς δεινόν τι οἰομένους πείσεσθαι εἰ ἀποθανοῦνται, ὥσπερ ἀθανάτων ἐσομένων ἂν ὑμεῖς αὐτοὺς μὴ ἀποκτείνητε· οἳ ἐμοὶ δοκοῦσιν αἰσχύνην τῇ πόλει περιάπτειν, [35b] ὥστ' ἄν τινα καὶ τῶν ξένων ὑπολαβεῖν ὅτι οἱ διαφέροντες Ἀθηναίων εἰς ἀρετήν, οὓς αὐτοὶ ἑαυτῶν ἔν τε ταῖς ἀρχαῖς καὶ ταῖς ἄλλαις τιμαῖς προκρίνουσιν, οὗτοι γυναικῶν οὐδὲν διαφέρουσιν. ταῦτα γάρ, ὦ ἄνδρες Ἀθηναῖοι, οὔτε ἡμᾶς χρὴ ποιεῖν τοὺς δοκοῦντας καὶ ὁπῃοῦν τι εἶναι, οὔτ', ἂν ἡμεῖς ποιῶμεν, ὑμᾶς ἐπιτρέπειν, ἀλλὰ τοῦτο αὐτὸ ἐνδείκνυσθαι, ὅτι πολὺ μᾶλλον καταψηφιεῖσθε τοῦ τὰ ἐλεινὰ ταῦτα δράματα εἰσάγοντος καὶ καταγέλαστον τὴν πόλιν ποιοῦντος ἢ τοῦ ἡσυχίαν ἄγοντος.

Why not? Not out of stubbornness, men of Athens, [34e] or disrespect for you. Whether I face death calmly or not is one thing. But my dignity, your dignity, and that of the city as a whole is another. Given my age and reputation, it would be unseemly for me to stoop to such behavior, especially since, rightly or wrongly, it's long been thought [35a] that Socrates is somehow *better* than most people. So if those of *you* who are thought to be better—wiser, more courageous, or greater in any other way—start acting like this, it would abase you. I've seen supposedly distinguished men abase themselves during trials like this many times, oddly acting as though death were the worst thing that could happen, as if they'd live forever if you'd only just spare them.[28] In my view, such people bring great shame on the city. [35b] Imagine what foreigners must think when they see the greatest of Athens' men—the ones they themselves select from among their ranks to rule and command—acting no better than women.[29] Men of Athens, those of us who are thought distinguished in any way ought not behave this way, and you should not tolerate it if we do.[30] Instead, you should make the point that you're far more inclined to vote *against* the man who stages these melodramatic scenes and makes a mockery of the

χωρὶς δὲ τῆς δόξης, ὦ ἄνδρες, οὐδὲ δίκαιόν μοι δοκεῖ [35c] εἶναι δεῖσθαι τοῦ δικαστοῦ οὐδὲ δεόμενον ἀποφεύγειν, ἀλλὰ διδάσκειν καὶ πείθειν. οὐ γὰρ ἐπὶ τούτῳ κάθηται ὁ δικαστής, ἐπὶ τῷ καταχαρίζεσθαι τὰ δίκαια, ἀλλ' ἐπὶ τῷ κρίνειν ταῦτα· καὶ ὀμώμοκεν οὐ χαριεῖσθαι οἷς ἂν δοκῇ αὐτῷ, ἀλλὰ δικάσειν κατὰ τοὺς νόμους. οὔκουν χρὴ οὔτε ἡμᾶς ἐθίζειν ὑμᾶς ἐπιορκεῖν οὔθ' ὑμᾶς ἐθίζεσθαι· οὐδέτεροι γὰρ ἂν ἡμῶν εὐσεβοῖεν.

μὴ οὖν ἀξιοῦτέ με, ὦ ἄνδρες Ἀθηναῖοι, τοιαῦτα δεῖν πρὸς ὑμᾶς πράττειν ἃ μήτε [35d] ἡγοῦμαι καλὰ εἶναι μήτε δίκαια μήτε ὅσια, ἄλλως τε μέντοι νὴ Δία πάντως καὶ ἀσεβείας φεύγοντα ὑπὸ Μελήτου τουτουΐ. σαφῶς γὰρ ἄν, εἰ πείθοιμι ὑμᾶς καὶ τῷ δεῖσθαι βιαζοίμην ὀμωμοκότας, θεοὺς ἂν διδάσκοιμι μὴ ἡγεῖσθαι ὑμᾶς εἶναι, καὶ ἀτεχνῶς ἀπολογούμενος κατηγοροίην ἂν ἐμαυτοῦ ὡς θεοὺς οὐ νομίζω.

ἀλλὰ πολλοῦ δεῖ οὕτως ἔχειν· νομίζω τε γάρ, ὦ ἄνδρες Ἀθηναῖοι, ὡς οὐδεὶς τῶν ἐμῶν κατηγόρων, καὶ ὑμῖν ἐπιτρέπω καὶ τῷ θεῷ κρῖναι περὶ ἐμοῦ ὅπῃ μέλλει ἐμοί τε ἄριστα εἶναι καὶ ὑμῖν.

city, than against a man who quietly upholds his dignity.

Reputation aside, gentlemen, I also don't believe it's [35c] right to beg a jury or try to escape conviction by begging, but rather to educate the jury and persuade it. A juror's role isn't to bestow favors based on personal appeals, but to determine what's appropriate and right. The juror has sworn his oath, not to show partiality to whomever he pleases, but to judge a case according to the law. We must not allow each other to get in the habit of violating that oath, because that wouldn't be pious of either of us.

So, men of Athens, don't expect me to behave toward you in ways that I believe are dishonorable or [35d] unjust or immoral in the eyes of the gods—especially not while I'm trying to defend myself against an accusation of impiety brought by Meletus here. You've sworn an oath, and if I were to manipulate and force you into acquitting me with emotional appeals, I'd clearly be teaching you *not* to believe in the existence of gods. And that would make my defense literally a self-accusation of disbelief in the gods.

But that's far from the truth. I do believe in them, men of Athens, as none of my accusers do. And I leave it to you and to the god to judge me in whatever way will be best for both me and you.

■ ■ ■

[35e] τὸ μὲν μὴ ἀγανακτεῖν, ὦ ἄνδρες Ἀθηναῖοι, [36a] ἐπὶ τούτῳ τῷ γεγονότι, ὅτι μου κατεψηφίσασθε, ἄλλα τέ μοι πολλὰ συμβάλλεται, καὶ οὐκ ἀνέλπιστόν μοι γέγονεν τὸ γεγονὸς τοῦτο, ἀλλὰ πολὺ μᾶλλον θαυμάζω ἑκατέρων τῶν ψήφων τὸν γεγονότα ἀριθμόν. οὐ γὰρ ᾤόμην ἔγωγε οὕτω παρ᾽ ὀλίγον ἔσεσθαι ἀλλὰ παρὰ πολύ· νῦν δέ, ὡς ἔοικεν, εἰ τριάκοντα μόναι μετέπεσον τῶν ψήφων, ἀπεπεφεύγη ἄν.

Μέλητον μὲν οὖν, ὡς ἐμοὶ δοκῶ, καὶ νῦν ἀποπέφευγα, καὶ οὐ μόνον ἀποπέφευγα, ἀλλὰ παντὶ δῆλον τοῦτό γε, ὅτι εἰ μὴ ἀνέβη Ἄνυτος καὶ Λύκων κατηγορήσοντες ἐμοῦ, [36b] κἂν ὦφλε χιλίας δραχμάς, οὐ μεταλαβὼν τὸ πέμπτον μέρος τῶν ψήφων.

τιμᾶται δ᾽ οὖν μοι ὁ ἀνὴρ θανάτου. εἶεν· ἐγὼ δὲ δὴ τίνος ὑμῖν ἀντιτιμήσομαι, ὦ ἄνδρες Ἀθηναῖοι; ἢ δῆλον ὅτι τῆς ἀξίας; τί οὖν; τί ἄξιός εἰμι παθεῖν ἢ ἀποτεῖσαι, ὅτι μαθὼν ἐν τῷ βίῳ οὐχ ἡσυχίαν ἦγον, ἀλλ᾽ ἀμελήσας ὧνπερ οἱ πολλοί, χρηματισμοῦ τε καὶ

■ ■ ■

The jury delivers a guilty verdict, and Meletus proposes the death penalty. Socrates now proposes the alternative punishment that the law allows him to.

[35e] I'm not angry at what has happened here, men of Athens, [36a]—that you've found me guilty. There are plenty of reasons why, but mostly because this outcome is what I expected. What does surprise me is how close the vote was. I didn't think the margin would be so small; I figured it would be larger. It seems now that if only thirty votes had gone the other way, I'd have been acquitted.

In fact, I'd say I have already been acquitted of Meletus's accusations—and not just acquitted, because it's clear to all that if it weren't for Anytus and Lycon joining in, [36b] he wouldn't have even secured the 20 percent minimum number of votes he needs to avoid the one thousand drachma fine.[31]

Now the man proposes the death penalty. Okay. So what alternate penalty should I propose for myself, men of Athens? Something appropriate, obviously? Well then, what? What is "appropriate" for me to suffer or pay simply because instead of living quietly, I spent my life neglecting the usual

οἰκονομίας καὶ στρατηγιῶν καὶ δημηγοριῶν καὶ τῶν ἄλλων ἀρχῶν καὶ συνωμοσιῶν καὶ στάσεων τῶν ἐν τῇ πόλει γιγνομένων, [36c] ἡγησάμενος ἐμαυτὸν τῷ ὄντι ἐπιεικέστερον εἶναι ἢ ὥστε εἰς ταῦτ' ἰόντα σῴζεσθαι, ἐνταῦθα μὲν οὐκ ᾖα οἷ ἐλθὼν μήτε ὑμῖν μήτε ἐμαυτῷ ἔμελλον μηδὲν ὄφελος εἶναι, ἐπὶ δὲ τὸ ἰδίᾳ ἕκαστον ἰὼν εὐεργετεῖν τὴν μεγίστην εὐεργεσίαν, ὥς ἐγώ φημι, ἐνταῦθα ᾖα, ἐπιχειρῶν ἕκαστον ὑμῶν πείθειν μὴ πρότερον μήτε τῶν ἑαυτοῦ μηδενὸς ἐπιμελεῖσθαι πρὶν ἑαυτοῦ ἐπιμεληθείη ὅπως ὡς βέλτιστος καὶ φρονιμώτατος ἔσοιτο, μήτε τῶν τῆς πόλεως, πρὶν αὐτῆς τῆς πόλεως, [36d] τῶν τε ἄλλων οὕτω κατὰ τὸν αὐτὸν τρόπον ἐπιμελεῖσθαι—

τί οὖν εἰμι ἄξιος παθεῖν τοιοῦτος ὤν; ἀγαθόν τι, ὦ ἄνδρες Ἀθηναῖοι, εἰ δεῖ γε κατὰ τὴν ἀξίαν τῇ ἀληθείᾳ τιμᾶσθαι· καὶ ταῦτά γε ἀγαθὸν τοιοῦτον ὅτι ἂν πρέποι ἐμοί. τί οὖν πρέπει ἀνδρὶ πένητι εὐεργέτῃ δεομένῳ ἄγειν σχολὴν ἐπὶ τῇ ὑμετέρᾳ παρακελεύσει; οὐκ ἔσθ' ὅτι μᾶλλον, ὦ ἄνδρες Ἀθηναῖοι, πρέπει οὕτως ὡς τὸν τοιοῦτον ἄνδρα ἐν πρυτανείῳ σιτεῖσθαι, πολύ γε μᾶλλον ἢ εἴ τις ὑμῶν ἵππῳ ἢ συνωρίδι ἢ ζεύγει νενίκηκεν Ὀλυμπίασιν· ὁ μὲν γὰρ ὑμᾶς ποιεῖ εὐδαίμονας δοκεῖν εἶναι, ἐγὼ δὲ εἶναι, καὶ ὁ μὲν

pursuits—like making money, running a household, military commands, leading the public, or all the other offices and conspiracies and factions that form in the city [36c]—and deciding instead that I'm just not radical enough to survive getting involved? I didn't get involved where I'd be of no benefit to you or myself. Instead, as I say, I got involved where I could do the greatest good. I went to each of you privately, urging you to prioritize caring for yourselves over your possessions, and to work on becoming the best and wisest version of yourselves. I also encouraged you to care less about the city's possessions than about the city itself [36d], and to approach everything else with the same attitude.

So what would be a fair punishment for someone like me? Surely something good, men of Athens, if I'm supposed to propose a penalty I truly deserve, and surely something good that's fitting and appropriate for *me*. So—what would be fitting for a poor man who's been a public benefactor of the city, and who needs time to continue exhorting you? What could be more fitting for such a man, men of Athens, than to be given free meals in the Prytaneum dining hall? It's certainly more fitting for him than for those of you who win Olympic victories in horse and team and chariot races. They make you feel happy, but I make you actually happy, and they

τροφῆς οὐδὲν δεῖται, [36e] ἐγὼ δὲ δέομαι. εἰ οὖν δεῖ με κατὰ τὸ δίκαιον τῆς ἀξίας τιμᾶσθαι, [37a] τούτου τιμῶμαι, ἐν πρυτανείῳ σιτήσεως.

ἴσως οὖν ὑμῖν καὶ ταυτὶ λέγων παραπλησίως δοκῶ λέγειν ὥσπερ περὶ τοῦ οἴκτου καὶ τῆς ἀντιβολήσεως, ἀπαυθαδιζόμενος· τὸ δὲ οὐκ ἔστιν, ὦ ἄνδρες Ἀθηναῖοι, τοιοῦτον ἀλλὰ τοιόνδε μᾶλλον. πέπεισμαι ἐγὼ ἑκὼν εἶναι μηδένα ἀδικεῖν ἀνθρώπων, ἀλλὰ ὑμᾶς τοῦτο οὐ πείθω· ὀλίγον γὰρ χρόνον ἀλλήλοις διειλέγμεθα. ἐπεί, ὡς ἐγῷμαι, εἰ ἦν ὑμῖν νόμος, ὥσπερ καὶ ἄλλοις ἀνθρώποις, περὶ θανάτου μὴ μίαν ἡμέραν μόνον κρίνειν ἀλλὰ πολλάς, [37b] ἐπείσθητε ἄν· νῦν δ' οὐ ῥᾴδιον ἐν χρόνῳ ὀλίγῳ μεγάλας διαβολὰς ἀπολύεσθαι.

πεπεισμένος δὴ ἐγὼ μηδένα ἀδικεῖν πολλοῦ δέω ἐμαυτόν γε ἀδικήσειν καὶ κατ' ἐμαυτοῦ ἐρεῖν αὐτὸς ὡς ἄξιός εἰμί του κακοῦ καὶ τιμήσεσθαι τοιούτου τινὸς ἐμαυτῷ. τί δείσας; ἦ μὴ πάθω τοῦτο οὗ Μέλητός μοι τιμᾶται, ὅ φημι οὐκ εἰδέναι οὔτ' εἰ ἀγαθὸν οὔτ' εἰ κακόν ἐστιν; ἀντὶ τούτου δὴ ἕλωμαι ὧν εὖ οἶδά τι κακῶν ὄντων τούτου τιμησάμενος; πότερον δεσμοῦ; καὶ τί με δεῖ ζῆν ἐν δεσμωτηρίῳ, [37c] δουλεύοντα τῇ ἀεὶ καθισταμένῃ ἀρχῇ, τοῖς ἕνδεκα;

don't need the food, [36e] but I do. So, if I'm supposed to propose a penalty fairly and according to what I deserve, [37a] then that's what I propose: free meals in the Prytaneum.

Maybe some of you think what I'm saying now is just as stubborn as my earlier refusal to beg for mercy. But that isn't the case, men of Athens—this is different. I'm convinced that I've never deliberately done anyone wrong.[32] I haven't been able to convince you of this, though, because we've only had a short time to talk with each other. Now, if you had a law allowing more than just a single day to decide a capital case, as other men do, I do believe [37b] you would have been convinced. But with so little time, it isn't easy to dispel deeply rooted prejudice.

Since I'm convinced I haven't done anyone wrong, I'm hardly going to wrong myself by suggesting that I deserve something bad and proposing that kind of penalty for myself. Why should I? Out of fear? But of what? Of suffering the penalty Meletus proposes, which I don't even know if it's a good thing or a bad thing? Should I instead choose one of the penalties I know are bad and propose that? Prison, for instance? But why? Why should I live in prison [37c], the slave of whichever group of overseers comes and goes into office?

ἀλλὰ χρημάτων καὶ δεδέσθαι ἕως ἂν ἐκτείσω; ἀλλὰ ταὐτόν μοί ἐστιν ὅπερ νυνδὴ ἔλεγον· οὐ γὰρ ἔστι μοι χρήματα ὁπόθεν ἐκτείσω.

ἀλλὰ δὴ φυγῆς τιμήσωμαι; ἴσως γὰρ ἄν μοι τούτου τιμήσαιτε. πολλὴ μεντἄν με φιλοψυχία ἔχοι, ὦ ἄνδρες Ἀθηναῖοι, εἰ οὕτως ἀλόγιστός εἰμι ὥστε μὴ δύνασθαι λογίζεσθαι ὅτι ὑμεῖς μὲν ὄντες πολῖταί μου οὐχ οἷοί τε ἐγένεσθε ἐνεγκεῖν τὰς ἐμὰς διατριβὰς καὶ τοὺς λόγους, [37d] ἀλλ᾽ ὑμῖν βαρύτεραι γεγόνασιν καὶ ἐπιφθονώτεραι, ὥστε ζητεῖτε αὐτῶν νυνὶ ἀπαλλαγῆναι· ἄλλοι δὲ ἄρα αὐτὰς οἴσουσι ῥᾳδίως; πολλοῦ γε δεῖ, ὦ ἄνδρες Ἀθηναῖοι. καλὸς οὖν ἄν μοι ὁ βίος εἴη ἐξελθόντι τηλικῷδε ἀνθρώπῳ ἄλλην ἐξ ἄλλης πόλεως ἀμειβομένῳ καὶ ἐξελαυνομένῳ ζῆν. εὖ γὰρ οἶδ᾽ ὅτι ὅποι ἂν ἔλθω, λέγοντος ἐμοῦ ἀκροάσονται οἱ νέοι ὥσπερ ἐνθάδε· κἂν μὲν τούτους ἀπελαύνω, οὗτοί με αὐτοὶ ἐξελῶσι πείθοντες τοὺς πρεσβυτέρους· [37e] ἐὰν δὲ μὴ ἀπελαύνω, οἱ τούτων πατέρες δὲ καὶ οἰκεῖοι δι᾽ αὐτοὺς τούτους.

ἴσως οὖν ἄν τις εἴποι· “σιγῶν δὲ καὶ ἡσυχίαν ἄγων, ὦ Σώκρατες, οὐχ οἷός τ᾽ ἔσῃ ἡμῖν ἐξελθὼν ζῆν;” τουτὶ δή ἐστι πάντων χαλεπώτατον πεῖσαί τινας ὑμῶν. ἐάντε γὰρ λέγω ὅτι τῷ θεῷ ἀπειθεῖν τοῦτ᾽ ἐστὶν καὶ διὰ τοῦτ᾽ ἀδύνατον ἡσυχίαν ἄγειν, [38a] οὐ πείσεσθέ

Should I be issued a fine and go to jail until I pay it? But that would be the same as what I just said, because I don't have the money to pay a fine.

What about exile? Maybe that's what *you* would propose for me, men of Athens, but I'd have to be gripped with a coward's love of life to be foolish enough for that. I can see that you—my fellow citizens—couldn't stand my conversations and discussions, [37d] and they've become so annoying and exhausting that you're now trying to get rid of them. Are other people going to find them easier to handle? Not a chance, men of Athens. Imagine what a wonderful life exile would be for me, a man of my age—wandering from one city to the next, finding myself forced to leave again and again! You see, I know full well that wherever I go, young people will gather to hear me speak as they do here. If I shoo them away, they'll get their elders to expel me. [37e] And if I don't shoo them away, their fathers and relatives will expel me to protect their young people.

Some of you might be wondering, "Socrates, couldn't we have you go live in exile if you'll just keep quiet and go about your life?" And that's the very hardest thing to convince some of you of. Because if I tell you that doing *that* would mean disobeying the god, and that my refusal to do so is why I *can't* just "go about my life," [38a] you won't believe

μοι ὡς εἰρωνευομένῳ· ἐάντ᾽ αὖ λέγω ὅτι καὶ τυγχάνει μέγιστον ἀγαθὸν ὂν ἀνθρώπῳ τοῦτο, ἑκάστης ἡμέρας περὶ ἀρετῆς τοὺς λόγους ποιεῖσθαι καὶ τῶν ἄλλων περὶ ὧν ὑμεῖς ἐμοῦ ἀκούετε διαλεγομένου καὶ ἐμαυτὸν καὶ ἄλλους ἐξετάζοντος, ὁ δὲ ἀνεξέταστος βίος οὐ βιωτὸς ἀνθρώπῳ, ταῦτα δ᾽ ἔτι ἧττον πείσεσθέ μοι λέγοντι. τὰ δὲ ἔχει μὲν οὕτως, ὡς ἐγώ φημι, ὦ ἄνδρες, πείθειν δὲ οὐ ῥᾴδιον.

καὶ ἐγὼ ἅμα οὐκ εἴθισμαι ἐμαυτὸν ἀξιοῦν κακοῦ οὐδενός. [38b] εἰ μὲν γὰρ ἦν μοι χρήματα, ἐτιμησάμην ἂν χρημάτων ὅσα ἔμελλον ἐκτείσειν, οὐδὲν γὰρ ἂν ἐβλάβην· νῦν δὲ οὐ γὰρ ἔστιν, εἰ μὴ ἄρα ὅσον ἂν ἐγὼ δυναίμην ἐκτεῖσαι, τοσούτου βούλεσθέ μοι τιμῆσαι. ἴσως δ᾽ ἂν δυναίμην ἐκτεῖσαι ὑμῖν που μνᾶν ἀργυρίου· τοσούτου οὖν τιμῶμαι.

Πλάτων δὲ ὅδε, ὦ ἄνδρες Ἀθηναῖοι, καὶ Κρίτων καὶ Κριτόβουλος καὶ Ἀπολλόδωρος κελεύουσί με τριάκοντα μνῶν τιμήσασθαι, αὐτοὶ δ᾽ ἐγγυᾶσθαι· τιμῶμαι οὖν τοσούτου, ἐγγυηταὶ δὲ ὑμῖν ἔσονται τοῦ ἀργυρίου οὗτοι ἀξιόχρεῳ.

■ ■ ■

me; you'll think I'm not being serious. If I then say it's the most important thing in the world for a human being to spend time every day discussing integrity and the other topics you hear me discussing and examining myself and others about—and for a human being, the unexamined life is not worth living—then once again, you'll find it even harder to believe me.[33] But this really is the truth, gentlemen, even though getting you to see it isn't easy.

At the same time, I'm not used to thinking of myself as deserving anything bad. [38b] If I had money, then I would've proposed a fine equal to what I could afford to pay—since that would have done me no harm. Since I don't, then if you want to fine me, fine me what I can afford. I suppose I might be able to pay a fine of one mina of silver. So that is what I propose.

Whisperings are heard behind Socrates's back.

... Hold on, men of Athens. Plato here and Crito and Critobulus and Apollodorus are telling me to offer thirty minae as a fine, and they agree to underwrite it. So I propose this amount, and these trustworthy gentlemen will guarantee the money.[34]

■ ■ ■

[38c] οὐ πολλοῦ γ' ἕνεκα χρόνου, ὦ ἄνδρες Ἀθηναῖοι, ὄνομα ἕξετε καὶ αἰτίαν ὑπὸ τῶν βουλομένων τὴν πόλιν λοιδορεῖν ὡς Σωκράτη ἀπεκτόνατε, ἄνδρα σοφόν—φήσουσι γὰρ δὴ σοφὸν εἶναι, εἰ καὶ μή εἰμι, οἱ βουλόμενοι ὑμῖν ὀνειδίζειν· εἰ γοῦν περιεμείνατε ὀλίγον χρόνον, ἀπὸ τοῦ αὐτομάτου ἂν ὑμῖν τοῦτο ἐγένετο· ὁρᾶτε γὰρ δὴ τὴν ἡλικίαν ὅτι πόρρω ἤδη ἐστὶ τοῦ βίου θανάτου δὲ ἐγγύς. [38d] λέγω δὲ τοῦτο οὐ πρὸς πάντας ὑμᾶς, ἀλλὰ πρὸς τοὺς ἐμοῦ καταψηφισαμένους θάνατον.

λέγω δὲ καὶ τόδε πρὸς τοὺς αὐτοὺς τούτους. ἴσως με οἴεσθε, ὦ ἄνδρες Ἀθηναῖοι, ἀπορίᾳ λόγων ἑαλωκέναι τοιούτων οἷς ἂν ὑμᾶς ἔπεισα, εἰ ᾤμην δεῖν ἅπαντα ποιεῖν καὶ λέγειν ὥστε ἀποφυγεῖν τὴν δίκην. πολλοῦ γε δεῖ. ἀλλ' ἀπορίᾳ μὲν ἑάλωκα, οὐ μέντοι λόγων, ἀλλὰ τόλμης καὶ ἀναισχυντίας καὶ

The jury votes for the death penalty. According to the ancient biographer Diogenes Laertius (2.42), eighty more jurors voted for the death sentence than had voted for the guilty verdict. If that is true and not legend (a big if, since Diogenes lived five centuries later), then Socrates's response proves that emotions can override reason so far that many of us will put a man to death—even if we believe he's innocent.

[38c] In return for a measly bit of time, men of Athens, you're going to earn a reputation and the blame from those who would vilify this city for killing Socrates—"a wise man." For even if I'm not wise, as they'll claim, those who wish to revile you will say so. If you'd waited just a little longer, this all would have happened of its own accord, since you can see my age and that I'm far along in life and close to death. [38d] (I say this not to all of you, but to those who voted to put me to death.)[35]

And to those same people, let me add this: perhaps you imagine I've been convicted, men of Athens, because I lacked the sort of arguments that might have persuaded you, had I thought it proper to do or say whatever it takes to avoid a penalty. Far from it. I was convicted not because I lacked arguments, but because I lacked the shamelessness and willing-

τοῦ μὴ ἐθέλειν λέγειν πρὸς ὑμᾶς τοιαῦτα οἷ᾽ ἂν ὑμῖν μὲν ἥδιστα ἦν ἀκούειν—θρηνοῦντός τέ μου καὶ ὀδυρομένου καὶ ἄλλα ποιοῦντος καὶ λέγοντος πολλὰ καὶ ἀνάξια ἐμοῦ, [38e] ὡς ἐγώ φημι, οἷα δὴ καὶ εἴθισθε ὑμεῖς τῶν ἄλλων ἀκούειν. ἀλλ᾽ οὔτε τότε ᾠήθην δεῖν ἕνεκα τοῦ κινδύνου πρᾶξαι οὐδὲν ἀνελεύθερον, οὔτε νῦν μοι μεταμέλει οὕτως ἀπολογησαμένῳ, ἀλλὰ πολὺ μᾶλλον αἱροῦμαι ὧδε ἀπολογησάμενος τεθνάναι ἢ ἐκείνως ζῆν.

οὔτε γὰρ ἐν δίκῃ οὔτ᾽ ἐν πολέμῳ οὔτ᾽ ἐμὲ οὔτ᾽ ἄλλον οὐδένα δεῖ τοῦτο μηχανᾶσθαι, [39a] ὅπως ἀποφεύξεται πᾶν ποιῶν θάνατον. καὶ γὰρ ἐν ταῖς μάχαις πολλάκις δῆλον γίγνεται ὅτι τό γε ἀποθανεῖν ἄν τις ἐκφύγοι καὶ ὅπλα ἀφεὶς καὶ ἐφ᾽ ἱκετείαν τραπόμενος τῶν διωκόντων· καὶ ἄλλαι μηχαναὶ πολλαί εἰσιν ἐν ἑκάστοις τοῖς κινδύνοις ὥστε διαφεύγειν θάνατον, ἐάν τις τολμᾷ πᾶν ποιεῖν καὶ λέγειν. ἀλλὰ μὴ οὐ τοῦτ᾽ ᾖ χαλεπόν, ὦ ἄνδρες, θάνατον ἐκφυγεῖν, ἀλλὰ πολὺ χαλεπώτερον πονηρίαν· [39b] θᾶττον γὰρ θανάτου θεῖ. καὶ νῦν ἐγὼ μὲν ἅτε βραδὺς ὢν καὶ πρεσβύτης ὑπὸ τοῦ βραδυτέρου ἑάλων, οἱ δ᾽ ἐμοὶ κατήγοροι ἅτε δεινοὶ καὶ ὀξεῖς ὄντες ὑπὸ τοῦ θάττονος, τῆς κακίας. καὶ νῦν ἐγὼ μὲν ἄπειμι ὑφ᾽ ὑμῶν θανάτου δίκην ὀφλών, οὗτοι δ᾽ ὑπὸ τῆς ἀληθείας ὠφληκότες μοχθηρίαν καὶ ἀδικίαν. καὶ ἐγώ τε τῷ τιμήματι ἐμμένω καὶ οὗτοι. ταῦτα μέν που ἴσως οὕτως καὶ ἔδει σχεῖν, καὶ οἶμαι αὐτὰ μετρίως ἔχειν.

ness to say or do whatever would have pleased you most—weeping and wailing and carrying on and making many other appeals that are beneath me. [38c] Such behavior is what you're accustomed to hearing from everyone else. But I didn't think that I should act in an unbecoming manner to escape danger then, and I don't now regret defending myself as I did. I would much rather defend myself as I did and die than act like that and live.

You see, neither in court nor in war should anyone—myself included—do [39a] anything and everything he can think of, and whatever it takes, to avoid death.[36] In battle, see, it's often clear that you can escape death by dropping your weapons and begging your pursuers for mercy. And there are many other tricks to avoid death in dangerous situations if one is willing to say or do anything. But evading death is not the hard thing, men of Athens; far harder is evading evil, [39b] since it runs faster than death. And now the slower runner has caught up to me, who am slow and old. Still, my accusers, quick and clever as they are, have been caught by the faster one—wickedness.[37] And though I depart now, condemned by you to die, they stand forever convicted of immorality and injustice by the truth. I accept my sentence, and so must they. Perhaps this is how things had to be, and I think it's fair that they are.[38]

[39c] τὸ δὲ δὴ μετὰ τοῦτο ἐπιθυμῶ ὑμῖν χρησμῳδῆσαι, ὦ καταψηφισάμενοί μου· καὶ γάρ εἰμι ἤδη ἐνταῦθα ἐν ᾧ μάλιστα ἄνθρωποι χρησμῳδοῦσιν, ὅταν μέλλωσιν ἀποθανεῖσθαι. φημὶ γάρ, ὦ ἄνδρες οἳ ἐμὲ ἀπεκτόνατε, τιμωρίαν ὑμῖν ἥξειν εὐθὺς μετὰ τὸν ἐμὸν θάνατον πολὺ χαλεπωτέραν νὴ Δία ἢ οἵαν ἐμὲ ἀπεκτόνατε· νῦν γὰρ τοῦτο εἴργασθε οἰόμενοι μὲν ἀπαλλάξεσθαι τοῦ διδόναι ἔλεγχον τοῦ βίου, τὸ δὲ ὑμῖν πολὺ ἐναντίον ἀποβήσεται, ὡς ἐγώ φημι. [39d] πλείους ἔσονται ὑμᾶς οἱ ἐλέγχοντες, οὓς νῦν ἐγὼ κατεῖχον, ὑμεῖς δὲ οὐκ ᾐσθάνεσθε· καὶ χαλεπώτεροι ἔσονται ὅσῳ νεώτεροί εἰσιν, καὶ ὑμεῖς μᾶλλον ἀγανακτήσετε. εἰ γὰρ οἴεσθε ἀποκτείνοντες ἀνθρώπους ἐπισχήσειν τοῦ ὀνειδίζειν τινὰ ὑμῖν ὅτι οὐκ ὀρθῶς ζῆτε, οὐ καλῶς διανοεῖσθε· οὐ γάρ ἐσθ' αὕτη ἡ ἀπαλλαγὴ οὔτε πάνυ δυνατὴ οὔτε καλή, ἀλλ' ἐκείνη καὶ καλλίστη καὶ ῥᾴστη, μὴ τοὺς ἄλλους κολούειν ἀλλ' ἑαυτὸν παρασκευάζειν ὅπως ἔσται ὡς βέλτιστος. ταῦτα μὲν οὖν ὑμῖν τοῖς καταψηφισαμένοις μαντευσάμενος ἀπαλλάττομαι.

[39e] τοῖς δὲ ἀποψηφισαμένοις ἡδέως ἂν διαλεχθείην ὑπὲρ τοῦ γεγονότος τουτουῒ πράγματος, ἐν ᾧ οἱ ἄρχοντες ἀσχολίαν ἄγουσι καὶ οὔπω ἔρχομαι οἷ ἐλθόντα με δεῖ τεθνάναι. ἀλλά μοι, ὦ ἄνδρες, παραμείνατε τοσοῦτον χρόνον· οὐδὲν γὰρ κωλύει διαμυθολογῆσαι πρὸς ἀλλήλους ἕως ἔξεστιν.

[39c] And now I would like to offer a prophecy to those of you who voted to convict me. After all, I'm at that moment when people are most inclined to prophesy—when they're about to die. To you gentlemen who are killing me, I say this: once I am gone, a far harsher punishment is surely coming for you than what you've inflicted by killing me. You did this in the belief it would free you from having to answer for your lives, but I tell you, it will have the opposite effect. [39d] There will be *more* people to challenge your beliefs—people I've been restraining till now, though you didn't notice—and they'll be even harder to handle because they're younger. You'll find yourselves more aggravated by them than you ever were by me, because if you think killing people will stop criticism of your misguided lives, you're mistaken. That's not getting rid of criticism—it's not even possible, much less honorable.[39] The easiest and most honorable way is not to silence others but to strive to live the best lives you can. This is my prophecy to those who voted to condemn me; and now, I am through with you.[40]

[39e] With those who voted to acquit me, however, I'd be happy to chat about what's transpired while the officials are occupied, and before I depart for the place where I must die. Stay with me these moments, gentlemen; there's no reason we can't exchange ideas while we still have the chance.

[40a] ὑμῖν γὰρ ὡς φίλοις οὖσιν ἐπιδεῖξαι ἐθέλω τὸ νυνί μοι συμβεβηκὸς τί ποτε νοεῖ. ἐμοὶ γάρ, ὦ ἄνδρες δικασταί—ὑμᾶς γὰρ δικαστὰς καλῶν ὀρθῶς ἂν καλοίην—θαυμάσιόν τι γέγονεν. ἡ γὰρ εἰωθυῖά μοι μαντικὴ ἡ τοῦ δαιμονίου ἐν μὲν τῷ πρόσθεν χρόνῳ παντὶ πάνυ πυκνὴ ἀεὶ ἦν καὶ πάνυ ἐπὶ σμικροῖς ἐναντιουμένη, εἴ τι μέλλοιμι μὴ ὀρθῶς πράξειν. νυνὶ δὲ συμβέβηκέ μοι ἅπερ ὁρᾶτε καὶ αὐτοί, ταυτὶ ἅ γε δὴ οἰηθείη ἄν τις καὶ νομίζεται ἔσχατα κακῶν εἶναι· [40b] ἐμοὶ δὲ οὔτε ἐξιόντι ἕωθεν οἴκοθεν ἠναντιώθη τὸ τοῦ θεοῦ σημεῖον, οὔτε ἡνίκα ἀνέβαινον ἐνταυθοῖ ἐπὶ τὸ δικαστήριον, οὔτε ἐν τῷ λόγῳ οὐδαμοῦ μέλλοντί τι ἐρεῖν. καίτοι ἐν ἄλλοις λόγοις πολλαχοῦ δή με ἐπέσχε λέγοντα μεταξύ· νῦν δὲ οὐδαμοῦ περὶ ταύτην τὴν πρᾶξιν οὔτ᾽ ἐν ἔργῳ οὐδενὶ οὔτ᾽ ἐν λόγῳ ἠναντίωταί μοι.

τί οὖν αἴτιον εἶναι ὑπολαμβάνω; ἐγὼ ὑμῖν ἐρῶ· κινδυνεύει γάρ μοι τὸ συμβεβηκὸς τοῦτο ἀγαθὸν γεγονέναι, καὶ οὐκ ἔσθ᾽ ὅπως [40c] ἡμεῖς ὀρθῶς ὑπολαμβάνομεν, ὅσοι οἰόμεθα κακὸν εἶναι τὸ τεθνάναι. μέγα μοι τεκμήριον τούτου γέγονεν· οὐ γὰρ ἔσθ᾽ ὅπως οὐκ ἠναντιώθη ἄν μοι τὸ εἰωθὸς σημεῖον, εἰ μή τι ἔμελλον ἐγὼ ἀγαθὸν πράξειν.

ἐννοήσωμεν δὲ καὶ τῇδε ὡς πολλὴ ἐλπίς ἐστιν ἀγαθὸν αὐτὸ εἶναι. δυοῖν γὰρ θάτερόν ἐστιν τὸ

[40a] I want to share with you, as friends, what I think this outcome might mean. You see, gentlemen of the jury—and you I can truly call "judges"—something amazing has happened to me. My usual harbinger, the angel's voice, has always been very active, often stopping me even over small matters if I was about to do something wrong. But now, with everything you see happening—what most people would consider the worst possible misfortune—the god's sign hasn't opposed me at all. [40b] It didn't stop me when I left the house this morning, or when I came here to court, or at any point during my speech as I was about to say something. Yet in past conversations it's intervened countless times, even in the middle of my speaking. But now it hasn't stopped me in anything I've done or said at any point in this affair.

Why do I think this has happened? I'll tell you: it seems to me that this outcome is probably something good, and that all of us [40c] who imagine death to be an evil must be wrong to think so. And now I have strong evidence for this, for there's no way my usual sign wouldn't have opposed me if I weren't about to do something good.

Let's also reflect in another way that there's plenty of reason to hope that death is something good.[41] After all, being dead is one of two things. Either it's

τεθνάναι· ἢ γὰρ οἷον μηδὲν εἶναι μηδὲ αἴσθησιν μηδεμίαν μηδενὸς ἔχειν τὸν τεθνεῶτα, ἢ κατὰ τὰ λεγόμενα μεταβολή τις τυγχάνει οὖσα καὶ μετοίκησις τῇ ψυχῇ τοῦ τόπου τοῦ ἐνθένδε εἰς ἄλλον τόπον. καὶ εἴτε δὴ μηδεμία αἴσθησίς ἐστιν, ἀλλ' οἷον ὕπνος, ἐπειδάν τις καθεύδων μηδ' ὄναρ μηδὲν ὁρᾷ, [40d] θαυμάσιον κέρδος ἂν εἴη ὁ θάνατος· ἐγὼ γὰρ ἂν οἶμαι, εἴ τινα ἐκλεξάμενον δέοι ταύτην τὴν νύκτα ἐν ᾗ οὕτω κατέδαρθεν ὥστε μηδὲ ὄναρ ἰδεῖν, καὶ τὰς ἄλλας νύκτας τε καὶ ἡμέρας τὰς τοῦ βίου τοῦ ἑαυτοῦ ἀντιπαραθέντα ταύτῃ τῇ νυκτὶ δέοι σκεψάμενον εἰπεῖν πόσας ἄμεινον καὶ ἥδιον ἡμέρας καὶ νύκτας ταύτης τῆς νυκτὸς βεβίωκεν ἐν τῷ ἑαυτοῦ βίῳ, οἶμαι ἂν μὴ ὅτι ἰδιώτην τινά, ἀλλὰ τὸν μέγαν βασιλέα [40e] εὐαριθμήτους ἂν εὑρεῖν αὐτὸν ταύτας πρὸς τὰς ἄλλας ἡμέρας καὶ νύκτας· εἰ οὖν τοιοῦτον ὁ θάνατός ἐστιν, κέρδος ἔγωγε λέγω· καὶ γὰρ οὐδὲν πλείων ὁ πᾶς χρόνος φαίνεται οὕτω δὴ εἶναι ἢ μία νύξ.

εἰ δ' αὖ οἷον ἀποδημῆσαί ἐστιν ὁ θάνατος ἐνθένδε εἰς ἄλλον τόπον, καὶ ἀληθῆ ἐστιν τὰ λεγόμενα, ὡς ἄρα ἐκεῖ εἰσι πάντες οἱ τεθνεῶτες, τί μεῖζον ἀγαθὸν τούτου εἴη ἄν, ὦ ἄνδρες δικασταί; εἰ γάρ τις ἀφικόμενος εἰς Ἅιδου, [41a] ἀπαλλαγεὶς τουτωνὶ τῶν φασκόντων δικαστῶν εἶναι, εὑρήσει τοὺς ὡς ἀληθῶς δικαστάς, οἵπερ καὶ λέγονται ἐκεῖ δικάζειν, Μίνως τε καὶ Ῥαδάμανθυς καὶ Αἰακὸς καὶ Τριπτόλεμος καὶ ἄλλοι

like being nothing at all, with no consciousness of anything whatsoever; or else, as people say, it's a kind of change—a relocation of the soul from here to another place. Now, if there's no consciousness, like a deep sleep where you don't even dream, [40d] then what an amazing improvement death would be! Because I suspect that if you had to choose a night on which you slept so soundly that you didn't even dream, and compare that night to all the other nights and days of your life—and then upon reflection had to say how many days and nights you'd spent in all your life that were happier or better, then I suspect anyone—and not just an ordinary person, but even the Great King of Persia—[40e] would find such nights rare compared to those other days and nights. So if that's what death is like, I for one call it an improvement, since all of time will seem no longer than a single night.

On the other hand, if death is more like a journey to another place, and the stories about it are true, and all who have died are there, then what greater good could there be, gentlemen of the jury? Imagine arriving in the world below, [41a] freed from these so-called judges here, and finding the true judges—the ones who are said to judge there—Minos and Rhadamanthus and Aeacus and Triptolemus, along

ὅσοι τῶν ἡμιθέων δίκαιοι ἐγένοντο ἐν τῷ ἑαυτῶν βίῳ, ἆρα φαύλη ἂν εἴη ἡ ἀποδημία;

ἢ αὖ Ὀρφεῖ συγγενέσθαι καὶ Μουσαίῳ καὶ Ἡσιόδῳ καὶ Ὁμήρῳ ἐπὶ πόσῳ ἄν τις δέξαιτ᾽ ἂν ὑμῶν; ἐγὼ μὲν γὰρ πολλάκις ἐθέλω τεθνάναι εἰ ταῦτ᾽ ἔστιν ἀληθῆ. [41b] ἐπεὶ ἔμοιγε καὶ αὐτῷ θαυμαστὴ ἂν εἴη ἡ διατριβὴ αὐτόθι, ὁπότε ἐντύχοιμι Παλαμήδει καὶ Αἴαντι τῷ Τελαμῶνος καὶ εἴ τις ἄλλος τῶν παλαιῶν διὰ κρίσιν ἄδικον τέθνηκεν, ἀντιπαραβάλλοντι τὰ ἐμαυτοῦ πάθη πρὸς τὰ ἐκείνων—ὡς ἐγὼ οἶμαι, οὐκ ἂν ἀηδὲς εἴη—καὶ δὴ τὸ μέγιστον, τοὺς ἐκεῖ ἐξετάζοντα καὶ ἐρευνῶντα ὥσπερ τοὺς ἐνταῦθα διάγειν, τίς αὐτῶν σοφός ἐστιν καὶ τίς οἴεται μέν, ἔστιν δ᾽ οὔ. ἐπὶ πόσῳ δ᾽ ἄν τις, ὦ ἄνδρες δικασταί, δέξαιτο ἐξετάσαι τὸν ἐπὶ [41c] Τροίαν ἀγαγόντα τὴν πολλὴν στρατιὰν ἢ Ὀδυσσέα ἢ Σίσυφον ἢ ἄλλους μυρίους ἄν τις εἴποι καὶ ἄνδρας καὶ γυναῖκας, οἷς ἐκεῖ διαλέγεσθαι καὶ συνεῖναι καὶ ἐξετάζειν ἀμήχανον ἂν εἴη εὐδαιμονίας; πάντως οὐ δήπου τούτου γε ἕνεκα οἱ ἐκεῖ ἀποκτείνουσι· τά τε γὰρ ἄλλα εὐδαιμονέστεροί εἰσιν οἱ ἐκεῖ τῶν ἐνθάδε, καὶ ἤδη τὸν λοιπὸν χρόνον ἀθάνατοί εἰσιν, εἴπερ γε τὰ λεγόμενα ἀληθῆ.

with all the other demigods who lived lives of justice in their time. Wouldn't that be an absolutely incredible journey?

And what about meeting Orpheus and Musaeus and Hesiod and Homer? How much would any of you give for *that* opportunity? I for one would gladly die many times over if those stories are true. [41b] For me, it would be amazing to spend time there—meeting Palamedes, and Ajax the son of Telamon, and anyone else from the past who met his death because of an unfair decision—and comparing my experiences with theirs. It would be utterly delightful. But the best part would be examining and questioning the people there, just as I do here, to find out who among them is truly wise and who only think they are. What would a person give, gentlemen, for the chance to question the leader [41c] of the great army to Troy, or Odysseus, or Sisyphus, or countless other men and women you could mention? Talking with them, spending time with them, and examining them there—wouldn't that be unimaginable happiness? And at least they don't put you to death down there for asking questions! Because besides being happier than we are here, they're already immortal for the rest of time—if, of course, the stories are true.[42]

ἀλλὰ καὶ ὑμᾶς χρή, ὦ ἄνδρες δικασταί, εὐέλπιδας εἶναι πρὸς τὸν θάνατον, καὶ ἕν τι τοῦτο διανοεῖσθαι ἀληθές, [41d] ὅτι οὐκ ἔστιν ἀνδρὶ ἀγαθῷ κακὸν οὐδὲν οὔτε ζῶντι οὔτε τελευτήσαντι, οὐδὲ ἀμελεῖται ὑπὸ θεῶν τὰ τούτου πράγματα· οὐδὲ τὰ ἐμὰ νῦν ἀπὸ τοῦ αὐτομάτου γέγονεν, ἀλλά μοι δῆλόν ἐστι τοῦτο, ὅτι ἤδη τεθνάναι καὶ ἀπηλλάχθαι πραγμάτων βέλτιον ἦν μοι. διὰ τοῦτο καὶ ἐμὲ οὐδαμοῦ ἀπέτρεψεν τὸ σημεῖον, καὶ ἔγωγε τοῖς καταψηφισαμένοις μου καὶ τοῖς κατηγόροις οὐ πάνυ χαλεπαίνω. καίτοι οὐ ταύτῃ τῇ διανοίᾳ κατεψηφίζοντό μου καὶ κατηγόρουν, [41e] ἀλλ᾽ οἰόμενοι βλάπτειν· τοῦτο αὐτοῖς ἄξιον μέμφεσθαι.

τοσόνδε μέντοι αὐτῶν δέομαι· τοὺς ὑεῖς μου, ἐπειδὰν ἡβήσωσι, τιμωρήσασθε, ὦ ἄνδρες, ταὐτὰ ταῦτα λυποῦντες ἅπερ ἐγὼ ὑμᾶς ἐλύπουν, ἐὰν ὑμῖν δοκῶσιν ἢ χρημάτων ἢ ἄλλου του πρότερον ἐπιμελεῖσθαι ἢ ἀρετῆς, καὶ ἐὰν δοκῶσί τι εἶναι μηδὲν ὄντες, ὀνειδίζετε αὐτοῖς ὥσπερ ἐγὼ ὑμῖν, ὅτι οὐκ ἐπιμελοῦνται ὧν δεῖ, καὶ οἴονταί τι εἶναι ὄντες οὐδενὸς ἄξιοι. [42a] καὶ ἐὰν ταῦτα ποιῆτε, δίκαια πεπονθὼς ἐγὼ ἔσομαι ὑφ᾽ ὑμῶν αὐτός τε καὶ οἱ ὑεῖς.

ἀλλὰ γὰρ ἤδη ὥρα ἀπιέναι, ἐμοὶ μὲν ἀποθανουμένῳ, ὑμῖν δὲ βιωσομένοις· ὁπότεροι δὲ ἡμῶν ἔρχονται ἐπὶ ἄμεινον πρᾶγμα, ἄδηλον παντὶ πλὴν ἢ τῷ θεῷ.

—ΤΕΛΟΣ—

But you too, gentlemen of the jury, should face death with confidence and remember this one truth: [41d] that nothing bad can happen to a good man, either in life or after death, and the gods do not neglect his troubles. This has not happened to me by accident. I see clearly that it was better for me to die now and be freed from my troubles. That is why the sign never stopped me, and I for one am not at all angry at those who condemned and accused me. This wasn't what they had in mind when they were condemning and accusing me; [41e] they hoped to harm me, and for that it's right to censure them.[43]

Still, I have one small request for them: when my sons grow up, gentlemen, punish them—give them grief as I've done to you if you see them caring more about money or anything else than integrity. If they think they're something when they're really nothing, rebuke them, as I have rebuked you, for failing to care for what they ought to and for thinking that they are something when they're really worth nothing. [42a] If you do this, then my sons and I will both have received just treatment from you.

But now it's time to go our separate ways—I to die, and you to live. Which of us is heading toward something better? That's unclear to all except the god.

—THE END—

THE GODS IN COUNCIL

LUCIAN

> We might ponder whether Socrates himself, as a tireless and annoying critic of his fellow Athenians, was a type of Momus figure.
>
> —GEORGE MCCLURE (2018, 7)

If Plato's *Apology* ask us to sympathize with the man or woman who refuses to conform, our bonus text flips the script. *The Gods in Council* asks how we'll act when we find ourselves at the helm of an institution that claims to champion free speech, only to be confronted by a member whose words push the limits. How will you handle things when free speech becomes so uncomfortable or repugnant that it crosses the line? Will you tolerate intolerance and allow blunt criticism? Or will you simply blunt criticism, and become illiberal to save liberalism?

Born five and a half centuries after Plato into the stability and safety of the Pax Romana, the author of this text, Lucian (c. 125–80 CE), was one of a kind. He lived in an era of superstition and bunkum and he saw through it all. Extraordinary claims and hucksters were popping up like mushrooms. Eager to expose charlatanry and champion skepticism over blind belief, Lucian lifted his pen and became the world's first prophet of common sense. He wanted readers to think for themselves—to question and

doubt and weigh claims against real-world evidence, and to be ever alert to hypocrisy and groupthink. And knowing that humor and irreverence slice through nonsense more cleanly than hectoring or reason ever will, he revived Plato's ancient art of the literary dialogue and sharpened its satirical twist.

Lucian went a step beyond Plato in another way, too. Plato had mythologized contemporary historical figures like Socrates to give his ideas universality and to shield himself from persecution by attributing them to a condemned figure. Lucian, even more cunningly, removes human conflict from planet earth entirely and displaces it onto the gods in heaven. By populating his dialogues with these mythological gods and heroes instead of real-world women and men, Lucian untethered his ideas from history and endowed them with a timeless universality.

George Orwell did something similar with *Animal Farm*. As he explains in the preface to the 1947 Ukrainian edition, "On my return from Spain [in 1937] I thought of exposing the Soviet myth in a story that could be easily understood by almost anyone and which could be easily translated into other languages." Lucian's goal of easy accessibility was similar, and it succeeded far beyond anything he could have imagined. In his time, he battered away at orthodoxy and pretension, gleefully mock-

ing the priests and mountebanks who made grand claims about the gods and the lifestyle gurus who ceaselessly preached virtue yet struggled to attain it. When Renaissance scholars rediscovered these works many centuries later and translated them into Latin, they reached new audiences disillusioned with the abuses of contemporary Christendom. Lucian's works thus helped fracture the Church during the Reformation and seeded the ideas of the Enlightenment, eventually culminating in the First Amendment.

By the Middle Ages, Christian writers were sure that Lucian was burning in hell for blasphemy. Curiously, however, he is not mentioned by a single contemporary during his lifetime. In other places and other times, writers have withheld their most incendiary thoughts, publishing them only posthumously. For all we know, Lucian may have done the same.

In any case, there's no doubt he was a lion of free speech. In a work titled *The Fisherman*, he parodies Plato's *Apology* to defend his irreverent style, even adopting the name "Parrhesiades"—essentially "Freespeechio"—for himself.

Our text here, *The Gods in Council*, is set on Mount Olympus. It begins with a practical problem in the celestial pantheon: overcrowding is driving up costs, eroding standards, and weakening heavenly

dignity. Interlopers are straining the system and sparking resentment—and worse, some are newly arrived, mixed-race "mongrels." Of course, saying this aloud was no more acceptable in polite society in Lucian's time than it would be now, so discontent is festering in silence. In a grand gesture of liberality, the sovereign Zeus, ever wise and benevolent, summons transparency to discover the undercurrents of unhappiness he's only hearing whispers of. He issues a sincere but naive guarantee of free speech for one and all—a contract, we might say, to hold tellers harmless in exchange for the truth—and instantly finds himself in over his head.

Lucian's mouthpiece in the dialogue is a minor god named Momus. Who is he? Before Lucian, nothing more than a name from a line in Hesiod's *Theogony*, an archaic epic poem on the genealogy of the Greek gods. In the primordial mists of time, says Hesiod, long before even Zeus existed, murky Night gave birth to "Momus"—a name we're meant to link to the verb *memphesthai*, meaning "to criticize." Inspired by this, Lucian presents Momus as the deity of blunt speech.

In 1792, the English barrister Thomas Erskine (1750–1823) defended Thomas Paine in absentia in London. Paine (1737–1809)—a Socrates of his times—had been charged with seditious libel for

publishing the second part of *Rights of Man*. Unlike Socrates, who refused to flee Athens under pressure, Paine had fled to France to avoid trial—and, in all likelihood, a lynching. "Constraint," declared Erskine, "is the natural parent of resistance, and a pregnant proof that reason is not on the side of those who use it." He then illustrated his contention with a garbled reminiscence of our dialogue (1793, 67–68):

> You must all remember, gentlemen, Lucian's pleasant story: Jupiter [Zeus] and a countryman were walking together, conversing with great freedom and familiarity upon the subject of heaven and earth. The countryman listened with attention and acquiescence, while Jupiter strove only to convince him; but happening to hint a doubt, Jupiter turned hastily around and threatened him with his thunder. "Ah! ha!" says the countryman, "now, Jupiter, I know that you are wrong; you are always wrong when you appeal to your thunder."

When you find yourself in charge, will free speech and transparency or paternalism and hypocrisy be the better policy? Lucian's dialogue will have you asking yourself that for days.

ΘΕΩΝ ΕΚΚΛΗΣΙΑ

ΛΟΥΚΙΑΝΟΥ

ΖΕΥΣ [1]: μηκέτι τονθορύζετε, ὦ θεοί, μηδὲ κατὰ γωνίας συστρεφόμενοι πρὸς οὓς ἀλλήλοις κοινολογεῖσθε, ἀγανακτοῦντες εἰ πολλοὶ ἀνάξιοι μετέχουσιν ἡμῖν τοῦ συμποσίου…

… ἀλλ᾽ ἐπείπερ ἀποδέδοται περὶ τούτων ἐκκλησία, λεγέτω ἕκαστος ἐς τὸ φανερὸν τὰ δοκοῦντά οἱ καὶ κατηγορείτω. σὺ δὲ κήρυττε, ὦ Ἑρμῆ, τὸ κήρυγμα τὸ ἐκ τοῦ νόμου.

THE GODS IN COUNCIL

LUCIAN

ZEUS [1]: All right, gentlemen—enough with the murmuring, the huddling, the whispering in corners. You're upset that too many "unwanted elements" have wormed their way into our celestial banquet.

*Uh-oh! The key word here—*ἀνάξιοι *(anaxioi)—literally means "unworthy," "undeserving," or "unfit." It's a potent, derogatory term used to dismiss others as unworthy of inclusion or privilege. Replace it with any ethnic or racial slur to feel its impact.*

Fine. This assembly has been convened to address that very issue, so let's have everyone speak their minds or make their accusations openly. Hermes, make the formal proclamation.

ΕΡΜΗΣ: ἄκουε, σίγα. τίς ἀγορεύειν βούλεται τῶν τελείων θεῶν οἷς ἔξεστιν; ἡ δὲ σκέψις περὶ τῶν μετοίκων καὶ ξένων.

ΜΩΜΟΣ: ἐγὼ ὁ Μῶμος, ὦ Ζεῦ, εἴ μοι ἐπιτρέψειας εἰπεῖν.

ΖΕΥΣ: τὸ κήρυγμα ἤδη ἐφίησιν· ὥστε οὐδὲν ἐμοῦ δεήσει.

ΜΩΜΟΣ [2]: φημὶ τοίνυν δεινὰ ποιεῖν ἐνίους ἡμῶν, οἷς οὐκ ἀπόχρη θεοὺς ἐξ ἀνθρώπων αὐτοῖς γεγενῆσθαι, ἀλλ᾿, εἰ μὴ καὶ τοὺς ἀκολούθους καὶ θεράποντας αὐτῶν ἰσοτίμους ἡμῖν ἀποφανοῦσιν, οὐδὲν μέγα οὐδὲ νεανικὸν οἴονται εἰργάσθαι.

ἀξιῶ δέ, ὦ Ζεῦ, μετὰ παρρησίας μοι δοῦναι εἰπεῖν· οὐδὲ γὰρ ἂν ἄλλως δυναίμην, ἀλλὰ πάντες με ἴσασιν ὡς ἐλεύθερός εἰμι τὴν γλῶτταν καὶ οὐδὲν ἂν κατασιωπήσαιμι τῶν οὐ καλῶς γιγνομένων· διελέγχω γὰρ ἅπαντα καὶ λέγω τὰ δοκοῦντά μοι ἐς τὸ φανερὸν οὔτε δεδιώς τινα οὔτε ὑπ᾿ αἰδοῦς ἐπικαλύπτων τὴν γνώμην· ὥστε καὶ ἐπαχθὴς δοκῶ τοῖς πολλοῖς καὶ συκοφαντικὸς τὴν φύσιν, δημόσιός τις κατήγορος ὑπ᾿ αὐτῶν ἐπονομαζόμενος. πλὴν ἀλλ᾿ ἐπείπερ ἔξεστιν καὶ

HERMES: Hear ye! Silence! Who among eligible gods wishes to address the assembly? The item on the agenda is a discussion ON THE STATUS OF FOREIGNERS AND IMMIGRANTS.

MOMUS: I, Momus, stand ready to speak—if I may, Zeus, sir.[1]

ZEUS: Your speech is already authorized by the proclamation—no further permission from me is needed.

MOMUS [2]: Very well. In that case, I say some of us (*glancing around the assembly, eyes sharp with accusation*) are acting outrageously. Not content with merely becoming gods instead of mortals, they feel their achievements mean nothing unless they get to bring their underlings and servants with them—and elevate them to our level as well.

And please do grant me full candor, Zeus, sir—I can offer no other. Everyone knows how free my tongue is. They know I cannot keep silent when things go amiss. I point out problems in everyone and everything, I say what I think loudly and unabashedly, and I do not hide my opinions out of fear or respect for anyone. Most of the gods find me so disruptive and unbearable that they call me "the public prosecutor." Yet since the proclamation—and

κεκήρυκται καὶ σύ, ὦ Ζεῦ, δίδως μετ᾽ ἐξουσίας εἰπεῖν, οὐδὲν ὑποστειλάμενος ἐρῶ.

[3] πολλοὶ γάρ, φημί, οὐκ ἀγαπῶντες ὅτι αὐτοὶ μετέχουσι τῶν αὐτῶν ἡμῖν ξυνεδρίων καὶ εὐωχοῦνται ἐπ᾽ ἴσης, καὶ ταῦτα θνητοὶ ἐξ ἡμισείας ὄντες, ἔτι καὶ τοὺς ὑπηρέτας καὶ θιασώτας τοὺς αὐτῶν ἀνήγαγον ἐς τὸν οὐρανὸν καὶ παρενέγραψαν, καὶ νῦν ἐπ᾽ ἴσης διανομάς τε νέμονται καὶ θυσιῶν μετέχουσιν, οὐδὲ καταβαλόντες ἡμῖν τὸ μετοίκιον.

ΖΕΥΣ: μηδὲν αἰνιγματῶδες, ὦ Μῶμε, ἀλλὰ σαφῶς καὶ διαρρήδην λέγε, προστιθεὶς καὶ τοὔνομα, νῦν γὰρ ἐς τὸ μέσον ἀπέρριπταί σοι ὁ λόγος, ὡς πολλοὺς εἰκάζειν καὶ ἐφαρμόζειν ἄλλοτε ἄλλον τοῖς λεγομένοις. χρὴ δὲ παρρησιαστὴν ὄντα μηδὲν ὀκνεῖν λέγειν.

ΜΩΜΟΣ [4]: εὖ γε, ὦ Ζεῦ, ὅτι καὶ παροτρύνεις με πρὸς τὴν παρρησίαν· ποιεῖς γὰρ τοῦτο βασιλικὸν ὡς ἀληθῶς καὶ μεγαλόφρον, ὥστε ἐρῶ καὶ τοὔνομα. ὁ γάρ τοι γενναιότατος οὗτος Διόνυσος ἡμιάνθρωπος ὤν, οὐδὲ Ἕλλην μητρόθεν ἀλλὰ Συροφοίνικός τινος ἐμπόρου τοῦ Κάδμου θυγατριδοῦς, ἐπείπερ ἠξιώθη τῆς ἀθανασίας,

you personally, Zeus, sir—have granted me full freedom to speak, I shall speak without any reservations.

[3] There are many here among us—let me repeat—who, despite their half-mortal origins, are far from content with getting to enjoy our councils and feasts as equals. They've brought their dependents and riffraff up here to heaven with them and exploited the system in registering them, and now they're receiving equal benefits and sharing our offerings, all without paying taxes.[2]

ZEUS: Enough speaking in code, Momus. Speak plainly and explicitly—name names. These vague accusations breed wild speculation, and everyone's playing guessing games about everyone else. As a champion of free speech, you ought hold nothing back.

MOMUS [4]: Bravo, Zeus, sir, for encouraging my candor! That is magnanimous—befitting a king of your stature. So I shall name the man: I am referring to our illustrious Dionysus here. He's a half-human mongrel—and through his mother, not even Greek. His mother's father, Cadmus, was some half-Syrian, half-Phoenician trafficker.[3] Now, since it was deemed necessary to grant this gentleman immortality, I'll say

οἷος μὲν αὐτός ἐστιν οὐ λέγω, οὔτε τὴν μίτραν οὔτε τὴν μέθην οὔτε τὸ βάδισμα· πάντες γάρ, οἶμαι, ὁρᾶτε ὡς θῆλυς καὶ γυναικεῖος τὴν φύσιν, ἡμιμανής, ἀκράτου ἕωθεν ἀποπνέων·

ὁ δὲ καὶ ὅλην φατρίαν ἐσεποίησεν ἡμῖν καὶ τὸν χορὸν ἐπαγόμενος πάρεστι καὶ θεοὺς ἀπέφηνε τὸν Πᾶνα καὶ τὸν Σιληνὸν καὶ Σατύρους, ἀγροίκους τινὰς καὶ αἰπόλους τοὺς πολλούς, σκιρτητικοὺς ἀνθρώπους καὶ τὰς μορφὰς ἀλλοκότους· ὧν ὁ μὲν κέρατα ἔχων καὶ ὅσον ἐξ ἡμισείας ἐς τὸ κάτω αἰγὶ ἐοικὼς καὶ γένειον βαθὺ καθειμένος ὀλίγον τράγου διαφέρων ἐστίν, ὁ δὲ φαλακρὸς γέρων, σιμὸς τὴν ῥῖνα, ἐπὶ ὄνου τὰ πολλὰ ὀχούμενος, Λυδὸς οὗτος, οἱ δὲ Σάτυροι ὀξεῖς τὰ ὦτα, καὶ αὐτοὶ φαλακροί, κεράσται, οἷα τοῖς ἄρτι γεννηθεῖσιν ἐρίφοις τὰ κέρατα ὑποφύεται, Φρύγες τινὲς ὄντες· ἔχουσι δὲ καὶ οὐρὰς ἅπαντες. ὁρᾶτε οἵους ἡμῖν θεοὺς ποιεῖ ὁ γεννάδας; [5] εἶτα θαυμάζομεν εἰ καταφρονοῦσιν ἡμῶν οἱ ἄνθρωποι ὁρῶντες οὕτω γελοίους θεοὺς καὶ τεραστίους;

ἐῶ γὰρ λέγειν ὅτι καὶ δύο γυναῖκας ἀνήγαγεν, τὴν μὲν ἐρωμένην οὖσαν αὐτοῦ, τὴν Ἀριάδνην, ἧς καὶ τὸν στέφανον ἐγκατέλεξε τῷ τῶν ἄστρων

nothing about him himself—or about that headband of his, or his constant drinking, or his unsteady gait. You all see him well enough: effeminate, a girly man, half out of his mind, reeking of alcohol all day long.

But the real outrage is that he's foisted his entire extended family on us. He's brought the whole merry band here—elevating Pan and Silenus and a gaggle of satyrs into gods. Crude, rowdy hicks, mostly goatherds, with weird physiques. Pan, for example, sports horns, a full beard, and looks like a goat from the waist down, so he's not all that different from an actual goat. Silenus is a bald old man with a snub nose, usually found slung over a donkey. He's from Lydia. The satyrs are bald too, with pointy ears and tiny budding horns like you see on kids. They're from Phrygia. Oh, and they have tails too. Do you see what sort of "gods" most-noble Dionysus has added to our ranks? [5] And when mortals see these absurd freaks, these "gods," we're shocked that they hold us in such contempt!

Oh, and I won't mention that Dionysus has brought a couple women up here too. First there's Ariadne, his mistress—he's admitted her *crown* to the starry heavens![4] Then there's

χορῷ, τὴν δὲ Ἰκαρίου τοῦ γεωργοῦ θυγατέρα. καὶ ὃ πάντων γελοιότατον, ὦ θεοί, καὶ τὸν κύνα τῆς Ἠριγόνης, καὶ τοῦτον ἀνήγαγεν, ὡς μὴ ἀνιῷτο ἡ παῖς εἰ μὴ ἕξει ἐν τῷ οὐρανῷ τὸ ξύνηθες ἐκεῖνο καὶ ὅπερ ἠγάπα κυνίδιον.

ταῦτα οὐχ ὕβρις ὑμῖν δοκεῖ καὶ παροινία καὶ γέλως;

ἀκούσατε δ᾽ οὖν καὶ ἄλλους.

ΖΕΥΣ [6]: μηδέν, ὦ Μῶμε, εἴπῃς μήτε περὶ Ἀσκληπιοῦ μήτε περὶ Ἡρακλέους· ὁρῶ γὰρ οἷ φέρῃ τῷ λόγῳ. οὗτοι γάρ, ὁ μὲν αὐτῶν ἰᾶται καὶ ἀνίστησιν ἐκ τῶν νόσων καὶ ἔστιν

“πολλῶν ἀντάξιος ἄλλων,”

ὁ δὲ Ἡρακλῆς υἱὸς ὢν ἐμὸς οὐκ ὀλίγων πόνων ἐπρίατο τὴν ἀθανασίαν· ὥστε μὴ κατηγόρει αὐτῶν.

ΜΩΜΟΣ: σιωπήσομαι, ὦ Ζεῦ, διὰ σέ, πολλὰ εἰπεῖν ἔχων. καίτοι εἰ μηδὲν ἄλλο, ἔτι τὰ σημεῖα ἔχουσι τοῦ πυρός.

εἰ δὲ ἐξῆν καὶ πρὸς αὐτὸν σὲ τῇ παρρησίᾳ χρῆσθαι, πολλὰ ἂν εἶχον εἰπεῖν.

ΖΕΥΣ: καὶ μὴν πρὸς ἐμὲ ἔξεστιν μάλιστα. μῶν δ᾽ οὖν κἀμὲ ξενίας διώκεις;

Erigone, the farm-girl daughter of Icarius. And the most ridiculous thing of all is that even the dog—yes, Erigone's *dog*—he's brought *it* up here too! I guess the poor girl wouldn't be happy in heaven without her little pet doggie.

What else can we call all this but an insult, alcoholism, and mockery?

But enough about Dionysus. Let me turn now to others—

ZEUS [6]: No, Momus. I can see where this is going—do not say a word about Asclepius or Hercules.[5] Asclepius is a doctor. He cures people of their illnesses; he's

"an indispensable powerhouse."[6]

And though Hercules is my son, he's earned his immortality through his labors. So I don't want to hear a word against either.[7]

MOMUS: I'll keep silent ... because of you, Zeus, sir—though I have plenty to say. I'll simply note in passing that they both still look a little ... singed.[8]

And I'd have plenty to say about you yourself, sir—if only I could speak freely—

ZEUS: Oh, for me, you're at complete liberty. You're not charging *me* with unlawful presence, are you?[9]

ΜΩΜΟΣ: ἐν Κρήτῃ μὲν οὐ μόνον τοῦτο ἀκοῦσαι ἔστιν, ἀλλὰ καὶ ἄλλο τι περὶ σοῦ λέγουσιν καὶ τάφον ἐπιδεικνύουσιν· ἐγὼ δὲ οὔτε ἐκείνοις πείθομαι οὔτε Ἀχαιῶν Αἰγιεῦσιν ὑποβολιμαῖόν σε εἶναι φάσκουσιν.

[7] ἃ δὲ μάλιστα ἐλεγχθῆναι δεῖν ἡγοῦμαι, ταῦτα ἐρῶ. τὴν γάρ τοι ἀρχὴν τῶν τοιούτων παρανομημάτων καὶ τὴν αἰτίαν τοῦ νοθευθῆναι ἡμῶν τὸ ξυνέδριον σύ, ὦ Ζεῦ, παρέσχες θνηταῖς ἐπιμιγνύμενος καὶ κατιὼν παρ᾽ αὐτὰς ἐν ἄλλοτε ἄλλῳ σχήματι, ὥστε ἡμᾶς δεδιέναι μή σε καταθύσῃ τις ξυλλαβών, ὁπόταν ταῦρος ᾖς, ἢ τῶν χρυσοχόων τις κατεργάσηται χρυσὸν ὄντα, καὶ ἀντὶ Διὸς ἢ ὅρμος ἢ ψέλιον ἢ ἐλλόβιον ἡμῖν γένῃ.

πλὴν ἀλλὰ ἐμπέπληκάς γε τὸν οὐρανὸν τῶν ἡμιθέων τούτων· οὐ γὰρ ἂν ἄλλως εἴποιμι. καὶ τὸ πρᾶγμα γελοιότατόν ἐστιν, ὁπόταν τις ἄφνω ἀκούσῃ ὅτι ὁ Ἡρακλῆς μὲν θεὸς ἀπεδείχθη, ὁ δὲ Εὐρυσθεύς, ὃς ἐπέταττεν αὐτῷ, τέθνηκεν, καὶ πλησίον Ἡρακλέους νεὼς οἰκέτου ὄντος καὶ Εὐρυσθέως τάφος τοῦ δεσπότου αὐτοῦ, καὶ πάλιν ἐν Θήβαις Διόνυσος μὲν θεός, οἱ δ᾽ ἀνεψιοὶ αὐτοῦ ὁ Πενθεὺς καὶ ὁ Ἀκταίων καὶ ὁ Λέαρχος ἀνθρώπων ἁπάντων κακοδαιμονέστατοι.

MOMUS: Worse, as Crete has it. There you can hear that said as well as another story about you—and they even have your tomb on display. Not that I believe them, any more than I believe the Aegians of Achaea about you being secretly swapped at birth as a baby.[10]

[7] But there is one matter I simply must speak to plainly: the origin of these abuses, Zeus, sir, is you. It is you who have bastardized our assembly. You set the precedent by your affairs with mortal women—appearing to them in one form or another to bed them. It has gone too far. We fear you'll get caught one day and sacrificed when you're a bull or melted down by some goldsmith when you're in gold form, and instead of Zeus we'll be left with nothing but a bracelet or necklace or earring.

The truth is that thanks to you, heaven is now swamped with these mongrels—there's no other way to say it. And the absurdity is surreal: suddenly Hercules has been elevated to godhood, while his boss, Eurystheus, is dead—and there's even a temple to "Hercules the slave" next to the tomb of Eurystheus—his master! Over in Thebes, meanwhile, Dionysus is divine, yet his cousins—Pentheus, Actaeon, and Learchus—are the most miserable mortals alive.

[8] ἀφ᾽ οὗ δὲ ἅπαξ σύ, ὦ Ζεῦ, ἀνέῳξας τοῖς τοιούτοις τὰς θύρας καὶ ἐπὶ τὰς θνητὰς ἐτράπου, ἅπαντες μεμίμηνταί σε, καὶ οὐχ οἱ ἄρρενες μόνον, ἀλλ᾽, ὅπερ αἴσχιστον, καὶ αἱ θήλειαι θεοί. τίς γὰρ οὐκ οἶδεν τὸν Ἀγχίσην καὶ τὸν Τιθωνὸν καὶ τὸν Ἐνδυμίωνα καὶ τὸν Ἰασίωνα καὶ τοὺς ἄλλους; ὥστε ταῦτα μὲν ἐάσειν μοι δοκῶ· μακρὸν γὰρ ἂν τὸ διελέγχειν γένοιτο.

ΖΕΥΣ: μηδὲν περὶ τοῦ Γανυμήδους, ὦ Μῶμε, εἴπῃς· χαλεπανῶ γὰρ εἰ λυπήσεις τὸ μειράκιον ὀνειδίσας ἐς τὸ γένος.

ΜΩΜΟΣ: οὐκοῦν μηδὲ περὶ τοῦ ἀετοῦ εἴπω, ὅτι καὶ οὗτος ἐν τῷ οὐρανῷ ἐστιν, ἐπὶ τοῦ βασιλείου σκήπτρου καθεζόμενος καὶ μονονουχὶ [9] ἐπὶ κεφαλήν σοι νεοττεύων, θεὸς εἶναι δοκῶν; ἢ καὶ τοῦτον τοῦ Γανυμήδους ἕνεκα ἐάσομεν;

ἀλλ᾽ ὁ Ἄττης γε, ὦ Ζεῦ, καὶ ὁ Κορύβας καὶ ὁ Σαβάζιος, πόθεν ἡμῖν ἐπεισεκυκλήθησαν οὗτοι, ἢ ὁ Μίθρης ἐκεῖνος, ὁ Μῆδος, ὁ τὸν κάνδυν καὶ τὴν τιάραν, οὐδὲ ἑλληνίζων τῇ φωνῇ, ὥστε οὐδ᾽ ἢν προπίῃ τις ξυνίησι;

τοιγαροῦν οἱ Σκύθαι ταῦτα ὁρῶντες, οἱ Γέται αὐτῶν, μακρὰ ἡμῖν χαίρειν εἰπόντες αὐτοὶ ἀπαθανατίζουσι καὶ θεοὺς χειροτονοῦσιν οὓς ἂν ἐθελήσωσι, τὸν αὐτὸν τρόπον ὅνπερ καὶ Ζάμολξις δοῦλος ὢν παρενεγράφη οὐκ οἶδ᾽ ὅπως διαλαθών.

[8] You see, Zeus, sir, once you opened the doors to such types and trained your eye on mortal women, everyone else has followed suit. And it's not just the men—you'll notice the goddesses are equally culpable. Anchises, Tithonus, Endymion, Iasion, and the others—all familiar figures—need no further comment; it would be tedious to dwell on them.

ZEUS: Not a word about Ganymede, Momus. I'll be angry if you disparage the young man's background and hurt his feelings.[11]

MOMUS: So does that mean ixnay on the eagle too? That it's up here in heaven—perched on your scepter, practically nesting on [9] your head—and passing for a god? Or are we giving that one a pass too, for Ganymede's sake?

In that case, Zeus, sir, what about Attis, Corybas, and Sabazius? How did those fellows end up heaped upon us? And that Mede, Mithras, in his caftan and cap—his Greek is so poor that if you toast "cheers!" over wine, he doesn't have a clue what you're saying.[12]

And so sizing all this up, the Scythians and Getae have snubbed us. They've gone into the god-making business themselves, voting immortality in heaven by the wave of a hand. That must be how a slave like Zamolxis got his name onto our register.[13]

[10] καίτοι πάντα ταῦτα, ὦ θεοί, μέτρια. σὺ δέ, ὦ κυνοπρόσωπε καὶ σινδόσιν ἐσταλμένε Αἰγύπτιε, τίς εἶ, ὦ βέλτιστε, ἢ πῶς ἀξιοῖς θεὸς εἶναι ὑλακτῶν; τί δὲ βουλόμενος καὶ ὁ ποικίλος οὗτος ταῦρος ὁ Μεμφίτης προσκυνεῖται καὶ χρᾷ καὶ προφήτας ἔχει; αἰσχύνομαι γὰρ ἴβιδας καὶ πιθήκους εἰπεῖν καὶ τράγους καὶ ἄλλα πολλῷ γελοιότερα οὐκ οἶδ' ὅπως ἐξ Αἰγύπτου παραβυσθέντα ἐς τὸν οὐρανόν, ἃ ὑμεῖς, ὦ θεοί, πῶς ἀνέχεσθε ὁρῶντες ἐπ' ἴσης ἢ καὶ μᾶλλον ὑμῶν προσκυνούμενα; ἢ σύ, ὦ Ζεῦ, πῶς φέρεις ἐπειδὰν κριοῦ κέρατα φύσωσί σοι;

ΖΕΥΣ [11]: αἰσχρὰ ὡς ἀληθῶς ταῦτα φὴς τὰ περὶ τῶν Αἰγυπτίων· ὅμως δ' οὖν, ὦ Μῶμε, τὰ πολλὰ αὐτῶν αἰνίγματά ἐστιν, καὶ οὐ πάνυ χρὴ καταγελᾶν ἀμύητον ὄντα.

ΜΩΜΟΣ: πάνυ γοῦν μυστηρίων, ὦ Ζεῦ, δεῖ ἡμῖν, ὡς εἰδέναι θεοὺς μὲν τοὺς θεούς, κυνοκεφάλους δὲ τοὺς κυνοκεφάλους.

ΖΕΥΣ: ἔα, φημί, τὰ περὶ Αἰγυπτίων· ἄλλοτε γὰρ περὶ τούτων ἐπισκεψόμεθα ἐπὶ σχολῆς. σὺ δὲ τοὺς ἄλλους λέγε.

ΜΩΜΟΣ [12]: τὸν Τροφώνιον, ὦ Ζεῦ, καὶ ὃ μάλιστά με ἀποπνίγει, τὸν Ἀμφίλοχον, ὃς ἐναγοῦς

[10] But that's not the worst of it, ladies and gentlemen. You—yes, you, the dog-faced fellow from Egypt in the linen vest—who might you be, exactly? And how do you hope to make it as a god with all that barking? And what about this spotted bull from Memphis—receiving salaams, delivering oracles, commanding priests? And I blush just thinking of the ibises and monkeys and goats and other preposterous creatures smuggled into heaven from Egypt. How can you stand to see them worshiped as equals—or worse, worshipped *more* than you, my fellow gods? And you, Zeus, sir—how can you tolerate having ram's horns planted on your head?[14]

ZEUS [11]: I agree—the conduct of these Egyptians is disgraceful. Still, Momus, much of it is symbolic and ritualistic. It's hardly fair for someone uninitiated to mock it.

MOMUS: Oh I agree, Zeus, sir—since we clearly need rituals to remind us that gods are gods and dogheads are dogheads.

ZEUS: Enough of the Egyptians for now—we'll revisit their case when time permits. Move on—and name the others.

MOMUS [12]: Trophonius, sir ... though the one that really sticks in my craw is Amphilochus.

ἀνθρώπου καὶ μητρολῴου υἱὸς ὢν μαντεύεται ὁ γενναῖος ἐν Κιλικίᾳ, ψευδόμενος τὰ πολλὰ καὶ γοητεύων τοῖν δυοῖν ὀβολοῖν ἕνεκα. τοιγαροῦν οὐκέτι σύ, ὦ Ἄπολλον, εὐδοκιμεῖς, ἀλλὰ ἤδη πᾶς λίθος καὶ πᾶς βωμὸς χρησμῳδεῖ, ὃς ἂν ἐλαίῳ περιχυθῇ καὶ στεφάνους ἔχῃ καὶ γόητος ἀνδρὸς εὐπορήσῃ, οἷοι πολλοί εἰσιν. ἤδη καὶ ὁ Πολυδάμαντος τοῦ ἀθλητοῦ ἀνδριὰς ἰᾶται τοὺς πυρέττοντας ἐν Ὀλυμπίᾳ καὶ ὁ Θεαγένους ἐν Θάσῳ, καὶ Ἕκτορι θύουσιν ἐν Ἰλίῳ καὶ Πρωτεσιλάῳ καταντικρὺ ἐν Χερρονήσῳ. ἀφ᾽ οὗ δ᾽ οὖν τοσοῦτοι γεγόναμεν, ἐπιδέδωκε μᾶλλον ἡ ἐπιορκία καὶ ἱεροσυλία, καὶ ὅλως καταπεφρονήκασιν ἡμῶν—εὖ ποιοῦντες.

[13] καὶ ταῦτα μὲν περὶ τῶν νόθων καὶ παρεγγράπτων. ἐγὼ δὲ καὶ ξένα ὀνόματα πολλὰ ἤδη ἀκούων οὔτε ὄντων τινῶν παρ᾽ ἡμῖν οὔτε συστῆναι ὅλως δυναμένων, πάνυ, ὦ Ζεῦ, καὶ ἐπὶ τούτοις γελῶ. ἢ ποῦ γάρ ἐστιν ἡ πολυθρύλητος ἀρετὴ καὶ φύσις καὶ εἱμαρμένη καὶ τύχη, ἀνυπόστατα καὶ κενὰ πραγμάτων ὀνόματα ὑπὸ βλακῶν ἀνθρώπων τῶν φιλοσόφων ἐπινοηθέντα; καὶ ὅμως αὐτοσχέδια ὄντα οὕτω

True son of a criminal outcast and a mother-murderer, he's out in Cilicia right now pretending to be a seer—spinning fabrications and peddling hope for a few coins. And that, Apollo, is why you no longer command the respect you once did. At this point, every stone or altar offers oracles as long as it's anointed, garlanded, and manned by a charlatan—and there's no shortage of them. The fevered seek cures at the statue of the athlete Polydamas in Olympia, and in Thasos they seek them at the statue of Theagenes. Over in Troy, they're sacrificing to Hector—and across the water in Chersonese, to Protesilaus.[15] Ever since our divine ranks started swelling with these impostors, temple robberies and perjury have surged. And respect? We've lost it—and rightly so.

[13] That's all I have to say about illegals and bastards. But I've also been hearing a raft of funny names—names for things that don't exist among us and never could—and honestly, Zeus, sir, I can't help but laugh at them. Where indeed is "Virtue," which we hear so much of? And show me "Nature" and "Destiny" and "Fortune"—if they aren't just idle names dreamed up by foolish philosophers, with no reality behind them. Yet these made-up names

τοὺς ἀνοήτους πέπεικεν, ὥστε οὐδεὶς ἡμῖν οὐδὲ θύειν βούλεται, εἰδὼς ὅτι, κἂν μυρίας ἑκατόμβας παραστήσῃ, ὅμως τὴν τύχην πράξουσαν τὰ μεμοιραμένα καὶ ἃ ἐξ ἀρχῆς ἑκάστῳ ἐπεκλώσθη. ἡδέως ἂν οὖν ἐροίμην σε, ὦ Ζεῦ, εἴ που εἶδες ἢ ἀρετὴν ἢ φύσιν ἢ εἱμαρμένην; ὅτι μὲν γὰρ ἀεὶ καὶ σὺ ἀκούεις ἐν ταῖς τῶν φιλοσόφων διατριβαῖς, οἶδα, εἰ μὴ καὶ κωφός τις εἶ, ὡς βοώντων αὐτῶν μὴ ἐπαΐειν.

πολλὰ ἔτι ἔχων εἰπεῖν καταπαύσω τὸν λόγον· ὁρῶ γοῦν πολλοὺς ἀχθομένους μοι λέγοντι καὶ συρίττοντας, ἐκείνους [14] μάλιστα ὧν καθήψατο ἡ παρρησία τῶν λόγων. πέρας γοῦν, εἰ ἐθέλεις, ὦ Ζεῦ, ψήφισμά τι περὶ τούτων ἀναγνώσομαι ἤδη ξυγγεγραμμένον.

ΖΕΥΣ: ἀνάγνωθι· οὐ πάντα γὰρ ἀλόγως ᾐτιάσω. καὶ δεῖ τὰ πολλὰ αὐτῶν ἐπισχεῖν, ὡς μὴ ἐπὶ πλεῖον ἂν γίγνηται.

ΜΩΜΟΣ: ἀγαθῇ τύχῃ. ἐκκλησίας ἐννόμου ἀγομένης ἑβδόμῃ ἱσταμένου ὁ Ζεὺς ἐπρυτάνευε καὶ προήδρευε Ποσειδῶν, ἐπεστάτει Ἀπόλλων, ἐγραμμάτευε Μῶμος Νυκτὸς καὶ ὁ Ὕπνος τὴν γνώμην εἶπεν.

have convinced the unthinking so thoroughly that no one bothers to sacrifice to us anymore. Everyone believes that regardless of how grand their offerings, "Fortune" will deliver what is "fated," what is individually "foreordained." So, Zeus, sir, I'd love to ask you: have you ever actually seen Virtue or Nature or Destiny anywhere? I can't be the only one who's always hearing about them in philosophers' debates—unless you, Zeus, sir, turn a deaf ear to their yammering.

I could say plenty more, but I'll stop here. I see that many are upset by what I've said—there's the booing and hissing, particularly from those stung by my candor. [14] So, to conclude: if you'll allow it, sir, I'd like to read out a motion on this matter—it's already drafted.

ZEUS: Go ahead. You make some good points, and we certainly do need to curb much of this before it spirals out of control.

MOMUS (*reading*): "*Good fortune upon us!* At a duly convened assembly on the seventh day of the month, Zeus presided as Chairman; Poseidon served as Vice Chairman; Apollo acted as Speaker; Momus, son of Night, was appointed Secretary; and Sleep proposed the following resolution:

ἐπειδὴ πολλοὶ τῶν ξένων, οὐ μόνον Ἕλληνες ἀλλὰ καὶ βάρβαροι, οὐδαμῶς ἄξιοι ὄντες κοινωνεῖν ἡμῖν τῆς πολιτείας, παρεγγραφέντες οὐκ οἶδα ὅπως καὶ θεοὶ δόξαντες ἐμπεπλήκασι μὲν τὸν οὐρανὸν ὡς μεστὸν εἶναι τὸ συμπόσιον ὄχλου ταραχώδους πολυγλώσσων τινῶν καὶ ξυγκλύδων ἀνθρώπων,

ἐπιλέλοιπε δὲ ἡ ἀμβροσία καὶ τὸ νέκταρ, ὥστε μνᾶς ἤδη τὴν κοτύλην εἶναι διὰ τὸ πλῆθος τῶν πινόντων·

οἱ δὲ ὑπὸ αὐθαδείας παρωσάμενοι τοὺς παλαιούς τε καὶ ἀληθεῖς θεοὺς προεδρίας ἠξιώκασιν αὑτοὺς παρὰ πάντα τὰ πάτρια καὶ ἐν τῇ γῇ προτιμᾶσθαι θέλουσι·

[15] δεδόχθαι τῇ βουλῇ καὶ τῷ δήμῳ ξυλλεγῆναι μὲν ἐκκλησίαν ἐν τῷ Ὀλύμπῳ περὶ τροπὰς χειμερινάς, ἑλέσθαι δὲ ἐπιγνώμονας τελείους θεοὺς ἑπτά, τρεῖς μὲν ἐκ τῆς παλαιᾶς βουλῆς τῆς ἐπὶ Κρόνου, τέτταρας δὲ ἐκ τῶν

WHEREAS many foreigners—Greeks and barbarians alike, being utterly unworthy of citizenship in our divine body politic—have, by means unknown, fraudulently gained access and are now treated as gods, so overcrowding heaven thereby that our banquet is packed with a disruptive rabble of random polyglot humanity; and

WHEREAS the supply of ambrosia and nectar has run dangerously low, driving up the price of a drink to a mina of silver due to increased consumption; and

WHEREAS these presumptuous interlopers have elbowed the ancient, true gods aside and, in contravention of all law and custom, claimed precedence for themselves, and furthermore claimed precedence in worship on Earth;

[15] THEREFORE BE IT RESOLVED by the Council and the Demos that an assembly be reconvened on Olympus on or about the winter solstice; that seven fully recognized gods be appointed as commissioners—three from the ancient Council of Cronus, and four from the

δώδεκα, καὶ ἐν αὐτοῖς τὸν Δία· τούτους δὲ τοὺς ἐπιγνώμονας αὐτοὺς μὲν καθέζεσθαι ὀμόσαντας τὸν νόμιμον ὅρκον τὴν Στύγα, τὸν Ἑρμῆν δὲ κηρύξαντα ξυναγαγεῖν ἅπαντας ὅσοι ἀξιοῦσι ξυντελεῖν ἐς τὸ ξυνέδριον, τοὺς δὲ ἥκειν μάρτυρας ἐπαγομένους ἐνωμότους καὶ ἀποδείξεις τοῦ γένους. τοὐντεῦθεν δὲ οἱ μὲν παρίτωσαν καθ᾽ ἕνα, οἱ δὲ ἐπιγνώμονες ἐξετάζοντες ἢ θεοὺς εἶναι ἀποφανοῦνται ἢ καταπέμψουσιν ἐπὶ τὰ σφέτερα ἠρία καὶ τὰς θήκας τὰς προγονικάς. ἢν δέ τις ἁλῷ τῶν ἀδοκίμων καὶ ἅπαξ ὑπὸ τῶν ἐπιγνωμόνων ἐκκριθέντων ἐπιβαίνων τοῦ οὐρανοῦ, ἐς τὸν Τάρταρον ἐμπεσειν τοῦτον.

[16] ἐργάζεσθαι δὲ τὰ αὐτοῦ ἕκαστον, καὶ μήτε τὴν Ἀθηνᾶν ἰᾶσθαι μήτε τὸν Ἀσκληπιὸν χρησμῳδεῖν μήτε τὸν Ἀπόλλω τοσαῦτα μόνον ποιεῖν, ἀλλὰ ἕν τι ἐπιλεξάμενον [17] μάντιν ἢ κιθαρῳδὸν ἢ ἰατρὸν εἶναι. τοῖς δὲ φιλοσόφοις [18] προειπεῖν μὴ ἀναπλάττειν κενὰ ὀνόματα μηδὲ ληρεῖν περὶ ὧν οὐκ ἴσασιν. ὁπόσοι δὲ ἤδη ναῶν ἢ θυσιῶν ἠξιώθησαν, ἐκείνων μὲν καθαιρεθῆναι τὰ ἀγάλματα, ἐντεθῆναι δὲ

Twelve, of whom Zeus shall be one; that said commissioners before convening swear the customary oath by Styx; that Hermes issue a proclamation summoning all claimants to our assembly; that said claimants present themselves with sworn witnesses and documentary proof of their status; that each claimant shall appear before the commissioners individually, and that upon review of each case the commissioners shall either declare them gods or deport them to their graves and family vaults; and that if any claimant so disqualified and permanently debarred by the commissioners is subsequently discovered setting foot in heaven, he shall be cast into Tartarus.

[16] Be it further resolved that each god ply his or her own craft—Athena shall not heal the sick, Asclepius shall not prophesy, and Apollo shall not combine so many different duties but will instead choose one, whether prophecy, music, or medicine; [17] that the philosophers be admonished not to invent meaningless names or spout nonsense about matters [18] they know nothing of; that any disqualified claimant already granted a temple or sacrifices shall see their statue removed and

ἢ Διὸς ἢ Ἥρας ἢ Ἀπόλλωνος ἢ τῶν ἄλλων τινός, ἐκείνοις δὲ τάφον χῶσαι τὴν πόλιν καὶ στήλην ἐπιστῆσαι ἀντὶ βωμοῦ. ἢν δέ τις παρακούσῃ τοῦ κηρύγματος καὶ μὴ ἐθελήσῃ ἐπὶ τοὺς ἐπιγνώμονας ἐλθεῖν, ἐρήμην αὐτοῦ καταδιαιτησάτωσαν.

τοῦτο μὲν ὑμῖν τὸ ψήφισμα.

ΖΕΥΣ [19]: δικαιότατον, ὦ Μῶμε· καὶ ὅτῳ δοκεῖ, ἀνατεινάτω τὴν χεῖρα· μᾶλλον δέ, οὕτω γιγνέσθω, πλείους γὰρ οἶδ᾽ ὅτι ἔσονται οἱ μὴ χειροτονήσοντες.

ἀλλὰ νῦν μὲν ἄπιτε· ὁπόταν δὲ κηρύξῃ ὁ Ἑρμῆς, ἥκετε κομίζοντες ἕκαστος ἐναργῆ τὰ γνωρίσματα καὶ σαφεῖς τὰς ἀποδείξεις, πατρὸς ὄνομα καὶ μητρός, καὶ ὅθεν καὶ ὅπως θεὸς ἐγένετο, καὶ φυλὴν καὶ φράτορας. ὡς ὅστις ἂν μὴ ταῦτα παράσχηται, οὐδὲν μελήσει τοῖς ἐπιγνώμοσιν εἰ νεὼν τις μέγαν ἐν τῇ γῇ ἔχει καὶ οἱ ἄνθρωποι θεὸν αὐτὸν εἶναι νομίζουσιν.

—ΤΕΛΟΣ—

replaced with that of Zeus, Hera, Apollo, or another proper deity, and the city shall instead provide a tomb and gravestone in lieu of an altar; and that failure to comply or refusal to present oneself before the commissioners shall result in default judgment."

That, ladies and gentlemen, is the resolution.

ZEUS [19]: A worthy motion, I'd say, Momus.— All in favor ... er—hold that thought. Those bound to vote "no" are clearly the majority, so ... the resolution is hereby *decreed!*

You are all dismissed. Once Hermes issues the proclamation, each of you must appear in person, along with solid proof of identity in multiple forms—father's name, mother's name, the reason and circumstances of your deification, and your tribal and clan affiliations. Anyone unable to produce such proof will learn that having a grand temple on Earth or being worshipped by mortals avails you nothing. The commissioners will not care.

—THE END—

Photograph of Denis Diderot's Socrates seal, from an autograph letter, dated September 21, 1779, addressed to Abbé Galliani in Naples. Sold as Lot 1469 by International Autograph Auctions Europe, S. L., Estepona, Spain, on June 19, 2025. Image used by permission.

A PARTING THOUGHT ON MORAL CERTAINTY

After a month in solitary confinement, Diderot gave in. Facing decades in prison, the thirty-five-year-old *philosophe* realized he was no Socrates. He confessed to writing those blasphemous and atheistic writings, agreed to refrain from undermining religion and morality in the future, and was released a couple months later.

Upon his return to freedom, Diderot recommenced work on his masterpiece, the famous *Encyclopédie*. The *Encyclopédie, or a Systematic Dictionary of the Sciences, Arts, and Crafts* was not some proto-Wikipedia, but a radical intellectual enterprise that would become both Bible and blueprint for the Enlightenment. The collective effort of many writers, it advanced the age's core ideals: reason, secularism, empirical inquiry, and the democratization of knowledge. And in keeping with the letter if not the spirit of the agreement he'd signed behind bars, Diderot salted its pages with sly irreverence, ironic barbs, and subversive digs at reigning pieties and

sacred systems anywhere he thought he could get away with it.

One relevant example is worth noticing here. In his article "Socratic Philosophy," Diderot—who by now had taken to sealing his correspondence with a signet depicting Socrates—wrote that Socrates "was accused of impiety, and it must be admitted that his religion was not that of his country. He scorned Greece's gods and superstitions. He had only pity for their mysteries. By the sheer force of his genius, he had risen to the knowledge of the oneness of God, and he had the courage to reveal this dangerous truth to his disciples." Accordingly, continued Diderot,

> The utter disgrace that has befallen those who found him guilty should encourage every free-thinker to speak the truth fearlessly.[1] It ought to prompt fashionable elites, who judge their own conduct so casually and criticize in us what they admire in Socrates, to be more consistent and circumspect. And it should strike fear into those whom Providence has charged with enforcing the laws and preserving the peace, by the thought that in the centuries to come, the [explanatory] systems they deem so venerable and impressive today will become,

> in the judgment of those who examine the absurdity of those systems dispassionately, nothing more than preposterous, contemptible mythology.

So much for "settled" questions! If nobody believes in the state religion of ancient Athens nowadays, implies Diderot, what might that suggest about the moral certainties and explanatory paradigms—including the state religion—of our own times? Because if we're living through an *omnium somnium* of our own—a crowd madness, a mass delusion, a craze—then surely only the heretics know it.

It was too much for Diderot's publisher. He quietly excised this incendiary passage from the page proofs before the book went to print. Down the memory hole it went, not to be rediscovered for some two hundred years—and only by accident.[2]

So although censorship works—indeed, it works all too well—perhaps it's fitting to close our volume with a glimmer of hope from the Roman historian Tacitus (56–c.120 CE). In 25 CE, under the increasingly authoritarian reign of Tiberius, the government had prosecuted a historian in a landmark free-speech trial. By praising the long-dead assassins of Julius Caesar, Aulus Cremutius Cordus had allegedly "harmed" the state or the emperor's sovereign

"majesty"—and that was treated as treason (*laesa majestas*). This was a first in Roman history, says Tacitus, a trumped-up charge, and though defiant, Cordus committed suicide under the pressure. The state then ordered his books to be burned.

Yet their efforts ultimately failed: some copies survived, hidden away in secret, later resurfacing. Reflecting on this irony, Tacitus smiles and remarks (*Annals* 4.35): "One can only laugh at the folly of those who think a ruling power can purge a memory even among future generations. On the contrary: punish an artist or writer, and his stature soars (*punitis ingeniis gliscit auctoritas*); and so foreign regimes—and all who practice the same brutality—bring only infamy on themselves and glory to their victims."

As all experience shows, the totalitarian impulse to muzzle dissent doesn't go away. So let's hope that all who occupy a position of authority will ponder Socrates's sobering words in *Apology* 39d: "If you think killing people will stop criticism of your misguided lives, you're mistaken. That's not getting rid of criticism—it's not even possible, much less honorable. The easiest and most honorable way is not to silence others but to strive to live the best lives you can."

ABOUT THIS EDITION

The Greek texts are those of the Loeb Classical Library editions, but I've divided Plato's text into shorter paragraphs, added stage directions based on implicit cues in the text and indications of speaker in the cross-examination scene, and preferred a single variant reading (ἡμᾶς for ὑμᾶς in 35b). I've also eased the punctuation in a few trivial places. As in most editions of Plato, passages are numbered by their traditional "Stephanus pages."

Lucian's Greek is easy enough to bring into English, but Plato's grammar and word order are so different that nothing like a word-for-word correspondence is possible (indeed, it would soon become misleading). Moreover, a few individual terms in the *Apology* call for special comment. One is the adjective *sophos* (σοφός), the root of "sophomore" and the name Sophia. Although I render *sophos* as "wise" and *sophia* as "wisdom," the Greek terms reach further than their English counterparts, and in ways that may surprise. They convey a kind of

practical and intellectual "savvy" that encompasses not only deep moral or political insight, but also technical "know-how" or artistic competence—whether in building a house or composing a song. (The Greek idea bears some resemblance to Howard Gardner's theory of "multiple intelligences.") And connected with *sophos* are two related nouns:

- *philosophos* (φιλόσοφος), which is best translated "freethinker" or "independent thinker." This term is complimentary in context and has none of the later Hellenistic or modern academic connotations associated with the word "philosopher"—the kind Lucian ridicules in section 13 of his dialogue. As Cicero famously remarked (*Academica* 15.1), "Socrates was the first to turn philosophy away from hidden matters and the mysteries of nature, which had preoccupied all philosophers before him. Instead, he brought philosophy into everyday life, focusing on questions of virtues and vices, and generally on what is good and bad."
- *sophistes* (σοφιστής). If *sophia* denotes wisdom or "intelligence," then a *sophistes*, the source of our words *sophisticated* and *sophistry*, is an "intellectual" in a disparaging, populist sense: a pundit or base rhetorician who pontificates

> widely with shallow knowledge and wins arguments, not with truth, but by sophistry—the exploitation of ambiguities, rhetorical tricks, and splitting hairs. Though the term appears only once in Plato's *Apology* (in 20a), its presence casts a long shadow. It slyly hints at the broader Athenian scorn for sophists in the fifth century BCE, and underscores the ironic possibility that Socrates himself might be seen as one.

Another crucial word in the *Apology* is the verb *nomizein* (νομίζειν), which appears in Meletus's complaint. Like "acknowledge," it is ambiguous. It can mean to either "believe in" the existence of the gods, or to "worship" them by the proper rites. One sense concerns thought, the other behavior. We can't tell which one the accusers intended, but Socrates plainly responds as if belief is at issue. If Meletus had originally meant worship, then Socrates's unscrupulous decision to treat the word as belief would be a shocking example of sophistry—one that would undermine the integrity of the whole defense. In that case, we would also expect Meletus to object in the cross-examination, yet he never does. For that reason, I've consistently translated it as "believe in."

A final matter calls for comment. As Socrates explains at length, in his boyhood he began hearing a "voice" that he alone could hear. For him, it's a good thing—a Spidey-sense that warns and stops him from following a misguided course of action. He characterizes this mysterious voice as a *daimonion* (δαιμόνιον). As a diminutive of *daimon* (δαίμων), "spirit," this word ought to mean "sprite"—which obviously conjures up the wrong image. There's no perfectly satisfying way to render the word in English, especially since Socrates implies—not necessarily truthfully—that this voice is the sole basis for Meletus's charge of idolatry. Over time, of course, the word *daimon* itself became the English word "demon." But since demons today are evil rather than benevolent or neutral, I've followed the lead of the Septuagint and the Renaissance *Life of Socrates* by Giannozzo Manetti (1396–1459) and rendered it "angel." Yes, it's too Christian, but it's better than every alternative (being, presence, visitant, apparition, ghost, genie) I could think of.

NOTES

Introduction

1 Quintilian, *The Education of the Orator* 9.2.27. Tacitus, the historian we'll meet at the end of this book, implies the Latin translation could also be *libertas* or *libido* (*Annals* 4.35).

2 *Poetics* 9, trans. Freeman (Aristotle 2022, 59–61).

3 *On the Style of Demosthenes* 23.

4 This treatise was falsely ascribed to the same Dionysius and has apparently never been translated. This and the quotations that follow come from section 8 (Usener and Radermacher 1904, 305).

5 United States Commission on International Religious Freedom, 2023.

6 Szasz 1976, 10–11.

7 In Hellenistic times (as early as the second century BCE), this word *kainós* (καινός) became indistinguishable

in some regions from the word *kenós* (κενός), meaning "vain" in the sense of "hollow, insubstantial, ineffective." It's impossible to tell when and where the two first came to sound identical, and hence whether Socrates's accusers or Plato himself ever meant to play on the two meanings. If they didn't, then the mere passage of time, *mirabile dictu*, added yet another layer of irony to Socrates's ordeal.

8 Preserved by Sextus Empiricus (second to third century CE) in *Against the Physicists* 9.54, the fragment was later cited and endorsed in *Theophrastus Redivivus* (vol. 1, 58), the massive clandestine anthology of atheism assembled in early modern France and the largest guide to atheism ever written. (The Latin original has never been translated.) Alas, when a jaded nobleman named Casimir Liszinski (Łyszczyński, 1634–89) reached the exact same conclusion twenty-one centuries later in Catholic Poland, his private writings were exposed and he was executed for impiety. The epitaph he'd planned was to announce "a truth that even those who know it teach is false: THE TEACHING OF THE WISE IS A PRUDENT LIE" (*doctrina sapientum prudens est mendacium*)—a Lucretian phrase laced with biblical irony (see Matthew 4:6). After elaborate expiatory rituals, his ashes were loaded into a cannon and shot toward "Tartary"—the lands of the infidel East (Adelung 1786).

9 Unfortunately for poor Meletus, to Greek ears his name sounds the way *Carey* does to ours—that is, it suggests a connection with the verb *meletan*, which means "to care" about something. As you'll see, Socrates exploits this pun ad nauseam.

10 Horace *Satires* 2.4.3, Ovid *Tristia* 5.12.12, and *Ibis* 559–60.

11 Szasz 2011, 42–43 (from September 1999).

The Apology of Socrates

1 Galileo (1564–1642), the father of modern science, was also seventy years old when he was tried and convicted before the Roman Inquisition in 1633, his recantation having failed to save him (he was kept under house arrest forever after). From his own prison cell in Naples, the Dominican heretic Tommaso Campanella (1568–1639) had penned in vain a protest on Galileo's behalf that bears repeating again and again (1622, 23): "Every group or law that forbids its followers to investigate the physical world should be suspected of falsehood" (*omnis hominum secta, aut lex, quae naturalium rerum investigationem suis vetat sequacibus, falsitatis nomine suspecta haberi debet*).

2 The playwrights are Aristophanes, Ameipsias, and Eupolis, but as will soon become evident, he mainly means

Aristophanes (c. 451–388 BCE). Twenty-four years earlier, Aristophanes had produced a brilliant anti-Socrates comedy called *The Clouds*. In it, both Socrates and a student at the school he runs declare, "There is no Zeus" (οὐδ' ἔστι Ζεύς). The play concludes when an exasperated father, convinced his son has been brainwashed, decides to "burn it all down." He sets fire to Socrates's school, the "Thinkery." (The play implies this is a bad idea.)

3 Ivy League students will recognize this mindset.

4 As explained in the section "About This Edition," "intellectuals" are the base rhetoricians known as "sophists."

5 "Mentor ... mental": Plato's pun is on *epistates* (mentor) and *epistemon* (expert).

6 Five minas of silver could purchase a high-quality slave—quite a sum, no doubt—but still significantly less than the hundred minas that the celebrity intellectual Protagoras had charged a generation earlier. The difference in cost is comparable to that between public and private universities in the United States.

7 The supporters of democracy had fled Athens upon the installation of The Thirty in 404 BCE but returned to power after they were overthrown the next year.

8 Socrates is trying to distinguish talent from genius. Schopenhauer later did so better: "Talent hits a target no one else can hit; genius hits a target no one else can

see" (1844, 391; translator unknown). Plato explores this theme more fully in his dialogue *Ion*.

9 Craftsmen specialize in a *techne*, a technique or skill in some technology (sculpting, furniture, digging ditches, and so on). Readers today may think of the Silicon Valley "tech bros" who excel in one domain, such as coding, and hence presume expertise in many others. (The formal name for such a person in English is *ultracrepidarian*.)

10 In 1619 the outspoken Carmelite freethinker Lucilio Vanini (1585–1619) of Naples was burned at the stake in Tolouse, but not before having his tongue torn out (an eyewitness says he "bellowed like a bull" in pain). Vanini was the first person in the Christian world to be executed for outright atheism rather than heresy, and his case caused a sensation. Looking back on it in a public lecture, the German lawyer and historian Peter Friedrich Arpe (1682–1740) quoted the charges against Socrates mentioned in this passage, noted their link to getting freethinkers and scientists suspected of atheism, and remarked (1712, 31): "You're still seeing the same scene play out, gentlemen, though the faces have changed: what happened to Socrates, the wisest of men, happened to Vanini" (*quod Socrati evenit viro sapientissimo, evenit Vanino*).

11 In 1985 and once again in 1988, the Canadian commercial artist Ernst Zündel (1939–2017) was prosecuted and convicted of Holocaust denial in Canada

and imprisoned in Germany. Although a private citizen, his two trials were criminal rather than civil affairs, and there is nothing else like them in North American history. The transcripts show how closely they reprised the trial of Socrates as Plato imagines it, from the charges and motives right down to the cast of characters. In his opening statement in the first trial, Zündel's attorney, Douglas Christie, offered a defense of free speech and inquiry that is strikingly similar to Socrates's defense here (Her Majesty the Queen v. Ernst Zundel [*sic*] 1985, 2345): "[Mr. Zündel] has made a diligent, honest search for the last twenty-five years to seek answers to questions that trouble him, questions that he conscientiously examined, that he thoroughly searched, not just in the ordinary sources that we can all watch [on] television, but he searched for eye witnesses, he searched for direct knowledge, he searched for truth and he concludes, after all his research, this is the truth." Years later Canada's Supreme Court agreed, vacated Zündel's conviction, and struck down as unconstitutional the "false news" law under which he'd been prosecuted.

12 A striking parallel to these charges appears in the Bible, and it (or rather the author, Luke) hints that in return for their outspokenness, early Christian evangelists might easily find themselves in a position as precarious as that of Socrates. In Acts of the Apostles—written, like

Plato's *Apology*, in Greek—Paul arrives in Athens on his missionary journey from God. He begins engaging one and all in dialogue in the very same marketplace where Socrates had done so five centuries earlier. One day, as Luke tells it (17:18–20):

> A group of Epicurean and Stoic philosophers began to debate with him. Some of them asked, "What is this babbler trying to say?" Others remarked, "He seems to be advocating foreign gods [*daimones*]." They said this because Paul was preaching the good news about Jesus and the resurrection. Then they took him and brought him to a meeting of the Areopagus, where they said to him, "May we know what this new [*kaine*—the same word as in Meletus's complaint] teaching is that you are presenting? You are bringing some strange ideas to our ears, and we would like to know what they mean."

Incidentally, fans of Stoicism will be intrigued to know that when the *Enchiridion* of Epictetus was adapted to Christian use by monks in Byzantine times—see the volume *How to Be Free* in this series—the name "Socrates" was changed to "St. Paul."

13 The secular reader today will gasp at these words and think Socrates's unexpected response too good to

be true. It isn't. Anaxagoras (c. 500–428 BCE) was a proto-scientist, and a generation before Socrates, he had indeed made these arguments. According to Xenophon (*Memories of Socrates* 4.7), Socrates had himself rebutted Anaxagoras's contentions by claiming that his view of the sun as fire ignored its unique effects: blinding light, the stimulation of vegetable growth, and perpetual brilliance. A drachma was 1/100th of a mina of silver (see note 6).

14 The point is rhetorically sharper in Greek than English since in Greek, the word for donkey is *onos*, and—as a hemisphere in English is "half" a sphere—the word for mule, *hemionos*, is literally a "half donkey."

15 *Iliad* 18.96.

16 A composite misquotation of *Iliad* 18.98 and 18.104 (with the rest made up by Socrates).

17 Socrates is referring to one's position in a standard Greek battle line, wherein "hoplite" soldiers stood shoulder to shoulder. The retreat of a single soldier in this formation could lead to the death of all his comrades.

18 These battles were fought in 432, 422, and 424 BCE, respectively.

19 This sentence inspired Lucian to compose a brilliant essay ridiculing the contradictions that arise from belief in life after death, or at least in hell (the essay concludes by quoting Socrates's words without attribution). Titled *On Funerals* in the Loeb edition and *Of Mourning*

in the Fowler translation (*De Luctu* in Latin, Περὶ Πενθοῦς in Greek), it remains well worth reading today. Shot through with irony, it is one of Lucian's most profound and challenging works—perfect for every freethinker out there.

20 Anytus meant that Socrates should have voluntarily gone into exile as soon as the charges were filed against him, but since he didn't, he should be put to death.

21 In 1486 the young freethinker Pico della Mirandola (1463–94) composed his *Oration on the Dignity of Man*, the "Manifesto of the Renaissance." Some think the current passage inspired his statement in section 150: "Freethought itself has taught me to rely on my own conscience rather than the opinions of others, and to worry less about being spoken badly of than about saying or doing anything bad myself." Pico died young, leaving behind a massive manuscript titled *Against the Astrologers* (published 1496). Although never translated, his proto-Enlightenment critique debunks astrology decisively, albeit from a Christian standpoint, and remains centuries ahead of its time.

22 These stirring words have echoed through the ages. When the Inquisition sentenced the Dominican freethinker Giordano Bruno (1548–1600) to burn for heresy, he replied, "You may be more afraid to pass this sentence on me than I am to receive it" (*Maiori forsan cum timore*

sententiam in me fertis quam ego accipiam). Today his statue stands in Campo de' Fiori in Rome facing the Vatican in defiance, and t-shirts bearing those words are sold at the Fahrenheit 451 bookshop nearby. Along the same lines, before he and his books were burned for heresy half a century earlier in Paris, the outspoken freethinker Étienne Dolet (1509–46) allegedly quipped "It is you pious folks, not Dolet, that suffer" (*non dolet ipse Dolet, sed pia turba dolet*). Of that, as Bruno might have said himself, *se no è vero, è ben trovato*: if it isn't true, it's at least a good story.

23 "*This* is the sound of justice!" exclaims Maximus of Tyre (late second century CE, *Oration* 12.8), while quoting this sentence to argue against our ever taking revenge: "And if everyone were to shout it from the rooftops, there'd be no more tragedies, no dramas on the stage, nor any of those countless, manifold disasters." Post-Socratic philosophers also made this sentence their mantra for shaking off the slings and arrows of outrageous fortune. It's the final sentence of the *Enchiridion* of the Stoic Epictetus, and Plutarch, a Platonist, cites it in *On Tranquility of Mind* (section 17). The sentiment was put to its most dramatic test much later, as documented in James Stockdale's 1993 book *Courage Under Fire: Testing Epictetus's Doctrines in a Laboratory of Human Behavior*. (Stockdale, a US vice admiral, was tortured mercilessly while captive in a North Vietnamese POW camp.)

24 This famous image of Socrates as the gadfly who stings complacency awake finds an echo in Giordano Bruno (see note 22), the freethinker whose own execution in Rome in 1600 is perhaps the nearest parallel to Socrates's trial in Western history. In happier days, Bruno had memorably styled himself "a shaker-awake of minds half-asleep" (*dormitantium animorum excubitor*). In similar fashion, in 2005 the German chemist Germar Rudolf (born 1964) was tried and imprisoned for Holocaust denial in Germany. In his defense speech, he quoted this passage and added (Rudolf 2012, 214–15): "Yes, for most people we [Holocaust] revisionists are a thorn in their flesh. We are pesky. We are a nuisance. We upset. We do not permit that society remains undisturbed in its complacency and illusion of infallibility. And this is a good thing." Rudolf was convicted, imprisoned, and his books burned under German police supervision.

25 Socrates is referring to a horrific scandal in Athenian history (a scandal from the time of the democracy, be it noted, rather than the reign of The Thirty). Seven years before his trial, in 406 BCE, Athens won a significant naval victory over Sparta in the Battle of Arginusae, off the coast of what is now Turkey. Though the victory was monumental, a storm later prevented the Athenians from rescuing their comrades stranded on disabled ships. The men drowned. This tragedy sparked widespread public outrage back home, resulting in a single trial for

the officers in charge. Six were found guilty and executed. There's a remarkable parallel here with Thomas Paine. After the monarchy in France was abolished and the Republic proclaimed, Louis XVI was put on trial and sentenced to death. Despite the danger Paine opposed the sentence, arguing for exile rather than execution, and for it he was subsequently arrested and imprisoned—and was only spared execution himself by a freak oversight.

26 The Rotunda (or "Tholos") served as the seat of government in Athens. Little more is known of poor Leon than what we can infer here, but Xenophon also condemns The Thirty for this incident in *Hellenica* 2.3.

27 An inexact quotation of *Odyssey* 19.163.

28 At the beginning of his speech Socrates said he'd never been in court before. Interpret that contradiction as you will.

29 It's impossible to overstate how pervasive sexism was in Athens in Socrates's time, where the bodies and movements of upper-class women were closely policed and a statesman such as Pericles could assert, to applause, that "the greatest glory for a woman is not to be spoken of at all, either for good or ill." (He says this in the famous funeral oration that Thucydides wrote for him.)

30 With a minority of editors, I prefer the suggestion "those of you" (*hymas*) over the manuscripts' "those of us" (*hemas*) simply because it makes more sense.

31 Socrates is apparently assuming (or pretending to assume) that the three accusers each got one-third of the 280 votes, and that 93 votes falls short of the requisite 100 of the 500 total.

32 At the sentencing stage of Ernst Zündel's first trial (see note 11), defense attorney Douglas Christie echoed Socrates on this point (Her Majesty the Queen v. Ernst Zundel [*sic*] 1985, Submissions on Sentence, 35–36): "My client maintains his honest belief, and I suggest that what was written and what he said, if he believes it, and he says he does, cannot justify remorse or sadness any more than someone who conscientiously believes an opinion which courts may find to be wrong can justify in their own conscience, saying, 'I'm sorry I believe this,' or, 'I'm sorry I say this or said this.' "

33 By appending "for a human being" to these timeless words, Plato is subtly signaling an etymological nudge—much as our rather less subtle finger-air quotation marks do when we speak a loaded term. In his dialogue *Cratylus* (399 c), he interprets the word for a human being (ἄνθρωπος, *anthropos*, the root of "anthropology") as a compound of ἀναθρῶν ἃ ὄπωπε (*anathron ha opope*), meaning "he who reflects on what he's seen." Socrates's implicit point is that the unexamined life is not worth living for "a human being *worthy of the name*."

34 This sum is hardly nothing—as noted above (note 6), it could buy six high-quality slaves.

35 This—the Streisand Effect—is a lesson that bad leaders never learn. If an offensive comedian's ratings are already falling, for example, it is counterproductive and stupid for the government to force him off the air. Just so, in 2008 the American Carmelite priest Reginald Foster (1939–2020) was interviewed on camera by comedian Bill Maher in front of St. Peter's Square in Vatican City, where Foster had served as papal secretary of Latin for forty years. Within moments it emerged that Foster—whose deportment evoked the habits of Socrates and the irreverence of Lucian—did not subscribe to the traditional tenets of Catholicism. He cheerfully dismissed beliefs in saints, ceremonies, Christmas, and even eternal damnation, which he called "that hell business." "These are all nice . . . stories, you know," he added. Shocked by his candor, Maher asked, half-jokingly, "So how do you convince people of what's the true faith?" "You don't," Foster replied: "Forget it. You just have to live and die with their stupid ideas." For this act of public impiety, several bishops complained to the pope. Unlike Socrates, however—and proving Socrates's point here—Foster was allowed to retire quietly rather than face dismissal, and the church successfully avoided a scandal. (The clip is available at https://www.youtube.com/watch?v=iTV-VgrbnZU&t=1s.)

36 Greek has no special vocabulary for legal terms, so the verb *diokein* means both "prosecute" and "pursue" and *pheugein* (and its compounds) means both "defend" and "avoid" or "escape" or "flee." Socrates exploits these ambiguities to spectacular rhetorical effect in this passage, but they're hard to translate.

37 "It runs faster than death" is crisp and alliterative in Greek—*thatton thanatou thei*—and may have been proverbial. By "evil" and "wickedness," I take Socrates to mean both self-betrayal or immorality and degradation. It is easier and faster to abandon one's principles and become a bad person than it is to die.

38 In 1416, the freethinking professor Jerome of Prague (c. 1365–1416) was burned at the stake for heresy. Poggio Bracciolini (1380–1459), a papal Latinist who later rediscovered Lucretius for Europe, was there in Konstanz and saw it. He reported the speech Jerome made in vain to defend himself, which began by referring to this passage of Plato's *Apology* (Foster and McCarthy 2016, 446—on Foster himself, see footnote 35): "He began by taking them back to Socrates, recounting how he was unjustly condemned by his fellow citizens. Despite having the chance to escape, Socrates refused, unwilling to evade the two things humans fear most: imprisonment and death."

39 In 1553, John Calvin had the freethinker Miguel Servetus (1509–53) burned at the stake for heresy and

blasphemy. A professor of Greek named Sebastian Castellio (1515–63) witnessed the burning and penned a response in horror. The most famous line in that response, *Against Calvin's Booklet*, echoes Socrates here (Plath 2019, 114–15):

> Killing a man is not protecting a doctrine, it is killing a man [*Hominem occīdere non est doctrinam tueri, sed est hominem occīdere*]. When the Genevans killed Servetus, they did not defend a doctrine, they killed a man. The defense of a doctrine is not the government's business (what does the sword have to do with doctrine?). It's the business of the teacher. The government's business is to defend the teacher the same way it defends the peasant, the artisan, the physician, and everyone else against injustices. If Servetus had wanted to kill Calvin, therefore, it would have been right for the government to defend Calvin. But since Servetus fought with arguments and writings, he should have been fought with arguments and writings.

In Basel today, the Latin sentence quoted above is displayed on a plaque inscribed in five languages.

40 In Greek, Socrates's final words "I am through with you" (*apallattomai*) repeat his words "getting rid

of" (*apallage*) a moment before: he is granting their wish and "cancelling" himself.

41 In the first century BCE, the Roman philosopher and statesman Cicero (106–43 BCE) translated this passage (*Apology* 40c–42a) into Latin and incorporated it into his *Tusculan Disputations* (1.97–99), a guide written to help college-age students live wise, happy, and meaningful lives.

42 A profound and epic troll—Aristophanes himself could not have written a wittier line. It is rhetorically sharper in Greek, where the word for "immortal" (*athanatos*) is more obviously the opposite of *thanatos* (death). In the Enlightenment, the atheist author of *Theophrastus Redivivus* (introduction note 8) took this passage as evidence that despite all his statements to the contrary, Plato merely professed belief in an afterlife out of fear of the masses (vol. 2, 621–22). And once again (see note 19), Lucian too was inspired by the line. In his essay *True History* (or *True Story*), he voyages to the Isles of the Blessed and finds Socrates there "shooting the breeze with Nestor and Palamedes," and surrounded by comely young men. He adds (2.17): "Word had it that Rhadamanthus was losing patience with Socrates, repeatedly threatening to banish him from the island if he wouldn't knock off the nonsense, drop the irony, and just enjoy himself for once."

43 The emphatic last word of this sentence, *memphesthai* (censure), is the verbal root of the name Momus and suggests the nature of his character. We'll meet him in Lucian's dialogue.

The Gods in Council

1 In 1897, the American humorist Mark Twain (1835–1910) wrote, "It is by the goodness of God that in our country we have those three unspeakably precious things: freedom of speech, freedom of conscience, and the prudence never to practice either." Twain—the American Lucian—practiced what he preached; his most heretical essays were discovered only after his death. Titled *Letters from the Earth*, the beginning is inspired by the current passage. God creates the cosmos from His throne in heaven. "At the end of an hour," Twain continues,

> the Grand Council [of archangels] was dismissed. They left the Presence impressed and thoughtful, and retired to a private place, where they might talk with freedom. None of the three seemed to want to begin, though all wanted somebody to do it. … At last the archangel Satan gathered his courage together—of which he had a very good supply—

and broke ground. He said: "We know what we are here to talk about, my lords, and we may as well put pretense aside, and begin."

2 The *metoikion* was an annual tax of twelve drachmas that resident foreigners in Athens had been required to pay in the time of Socrates. It no longer existed in Lucian's time.

3 Momus does not mention what everyone knows: that Dionysus's father is Zeus himself. (His mother was a mortal woman named Semele.)

4 The Corona Borealis.

5 Asclepius was the son of Apollo and a mortal woman named Coronis. He was so successful as a healer that he began bringing the dead back to life. This was a big no-no, so Zeus slew him with a lightning bolt, but made him immortal at Apollo's request.

6 *Iliad* 11.514. The phrase is used of Machaon, army medic in the Trojan War, and subsequently became proverbial praise for doctors.

7 Hercules's mother was Alcmene, a mortal. After completing his twelve labors, and suffering from a poisoned garment given to him by his wife, he sought to end his agony by suicide. He built a funeral pyre and was consumed by flames, but Zeus raised his soul to godhood.

8 This fillip has a double point, because slaves in ancient Greece and Rome could be branded like cattle.

9 Another Athenian law from long before Lucian's time. In classical Athens, anyone caught usurping the rights of citizenship could be charged with the crime named here, a *graphe xenias*.

10 The king of the gods should of course not have a tomb, but many ancient writers mention a tomb of Zeus in Crete. In the city of Aegium, Lucian's travel-guide-writing contemporary Pausanias saw a bronze statue of Zeus depicted as a boy (*Description of Greece* 7.24.4).

11 Ganymede was a mortal boy in Troy. Smitten by lust, Zeus abducted him in eagle form to serve him in heaven. Reflecting this role, in time his name became the English word "catamite," which is the old-fashioned name for the underage victim of a pederast. (The only such word in modern English is *bacha bāzī*, a borrowing from languages spoken in Afghanistan.) Lucian was horrified by Greek pederasty, which the myth of Ganymede was devised to explain.

12 Various "weirdo" gods were associated with charismatic or voodoo rites, some quite popular in Lucian's time, and all of them originated from somewhere "out there" in the mysterious East.

13 Zamolxis was an early charlatan man-god, and his impostures are not to be missed (Herodotus reports them in *Histories* 4.94–96). In a discussion of the origins of

Islam, this paragraph of Lucian is quoted in *Theophrastus Redivivus* (vol. 2, 525; see introduction note 8).

14 The dog is Anubis, the bull Apis, and the ram Ammon (also called Zeus Ammon).

15 Thracian Chersonese, the modern Gallipoli Peninsula of Turkey.

A Parting Thought on Moral Certainty

1 Diderot doesn't say so, but no less than the Roman Emperor Marcus Aurelius (121–80 CE) had called those who found Socrates guilty "vermin" (*phtheires*) in his Stoic-inflected *Meditations* (3.3).

2 The passage is printed in Gordon and Torrey 1947.

BIBLIOGRAPHY

For more on the historical context of Socrates's trial and execution, readers are warmly directed to Waterfield 2009. Henderson 1998 and Saxonhouse 2006 are superb overviews of free speech in fifth-century Athens, and Werhan 2008 lays out similarities and differences between the Athenian and American conceptions. Michel Foucault's six lectures on parrhesia are among the more comprehensible and reliable things he wrote and remain well worth reading. They are available online at https://foucault.info/parrhesia//.

Those interested in exploring more of Lucian's works should turn to the translation by Fowler and Fowler, which is widely available online. Their prose style, reminiscent of Mark Twain, more than compensates for the small liberties they take with the text. A good place to start is Lucian's dialogue Hermotimus, *which might be retitled* How to Have Common Sense *in English. Hilarious in its own right, it became the basis for Erasmus's* Praise

of Folly. *Marsh 1998 is an excellent introduction to Lucian's influence on the Reformation, and Gay 1970 to his influence on the Enlightenment.*

Bury 1913 is an excellent introduction to free-thought through the ages, and warmly recommended.

Adelung, Johann Christoph. 1786. *Geschichte der menschlichen Narrheit.* Vol. 2. Weygand.

Aristotle. 2022. *How to Tell a Story: An Ancient Guide to the Art of Storytelling for Writers and Readers.* Translated by Philip Freeman. Princeton University Press.

Arpe, Peter Franz. 1712. *Apologia pro Jul. Caesare Vanino neapolitano.* Typis Philaletheis.

Bury, J. B. 1913. *A History of Freedom of Thought.* Henry Holt & Company.

Campanella, Thomas. 1622. *Apologia pro Galileo.* Frankfurt.

Diderot, Denis. 1978. *Apologie de Socrate.* Edited and commented by Raymond Trousson. In *Œuvres complètes de Diderot*, vol. 4, 235–81. Hermann.

Erskine, Thomas. 1793. *The Celebrated Speech of the Hon. T. Erskine in Support of the Liberty of the Press: Delivered at Guildhall, December 18, 1792.* John Buel.

Foster, Reginald Thomas, and Daniel P. McCarthy. 2016. *Ossa Latinitatis Sola ad Mentem Reginaldi Rationemque.* Catholic University of America Press.

Gay, Peter. 1970. *The Bridge of Criticism: Dialogues Among Lucian, Erasmus, and Voltaire on the Enlightenment*. Harper & Row.

Gordon, Douglas H., and Norman L. Torrey. 1947. *The Censoring of Diderot's Encyclopédie and the Re-established Text.* Columbia University Press.

Henderson, Jeffrey. 1998. "Attic Old Comedy, Frank Speech, and Democracy." In *Democracy, Empire, and the Arts in Fifth-Century Athens*, edited by Deborah Boedeker and Kurt A. Raaflaub, 255–73. Harvard University Press.

Her Majesty the Queen v. Ernst Zundel [*sic*]. 1985. Court transcript, Toronto: District Court of Ontario. Appearances: Peter Griffiths, esq., for the Crown, and Douglas Christie, esq., for the accused. January 7. http://tinyurl.com/ZundelTrial.

Lucian of Samosata. 1936. *The Passing of Peregrinus. The Runaways. Toxaris or Friendship. The Dance. Lexiphanes. The Eunuch. Astrology. The Mistaken Critic. The Parliament of the Gods. The Tyrannicide. Disowned.* Translated by A. M. Harmon. Loeb Classical Library 302. Harvard University Press.

Marsh, David. 1998. *Lucian and the Latins: Humor and Humanism in the Early Renaissance*. University of Michigan Press.

McClure, George. 2018. *Doubting the Divine in Early Modern Europe: The Revival of Momus, the Agnostic

God. Cambridge University Press.

Plath, Ulrich, ed. 2019. *Sebastian Castellio, Contra libellum Calvini: A New Critical Edition Supplemented by the Text of the Basle Manuscript-Fragment.* Librairie Droz.

Plato. 2017. *Euthyphro. Apology. Crito. Phaedo.* Edited and translated by Chris Emlyn-Jones and William Preddy. Loeb Classical Library 36. Harvard University Press.

Rudolf, Germar. 2012. *Resistance Is Obligatory: Address to the Mannheim District Court, 15 November 2006 to 29 January 2007.* Castle Hill Publishers.

Saxonhouse, Arlene W. 2006. *Free Speech and Democracy in Ancient Athens.* Cambridge University Press.

Schopenhauer, Arthur. 1819. *Die Welt als Wille und Vorstellung* [*The World as Will and Representation*]. Vol. 1. Leipzig.

Schopenhauer, Arthur. 1844. *Die Welt als Wille und Vorstellung* [*The World as Will and Representation*]. Vol. 2. Leipzig.

Szasz, Thomas. 1976. *Heresies.* Anchor Books.

Szasz, Thomas. 2011. *The Szasz Quotationary: The Wit and Wisdom of Thomas Szasz.* Edited by Linda R. Frank. Kindle.

Theophrastus Redivivus. 1981–82. Edited by Gian Mario Canziani and Giovanni Paganini. Vols. 1–2. La Nuova Italia.

United States Commission on International Religious Freedom. 2023. "Legislation Factsheet: Blasphemy (2023 Update)." September. Retrieved from https://www.uscirf.gov/sites/default/files/2023-09/2023%20Blasphemy%20Legislation%20Factsheet.pdf.

Usener, Hermann, and Ludwig Radermacher, eds. 1904. *Dionysii Halicarnasei Opuscula.* Vol. 2. Teubner.

Waterfield, Robin. 2009. *Why Socrates Died: Dispelling the Myths.* Norton.

Werhan, Keith. 2008. "The Athenian Ancestry of American Freedom of Speech." *Supreme Court Review*, vol. 2008, no. 1: 293–347.